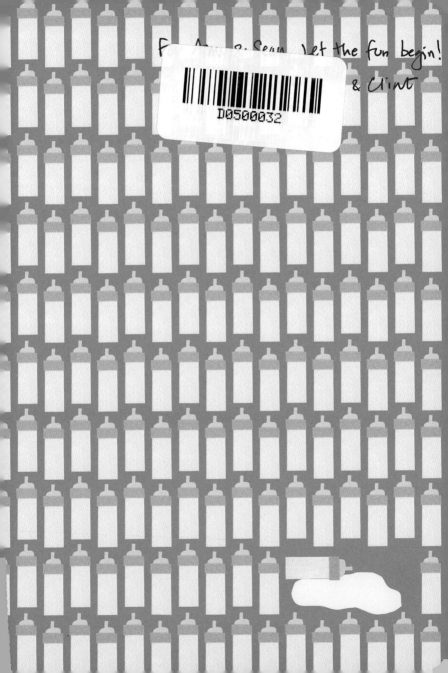

For ~~Anne & Sean~~ let the fun begin!

& Clint

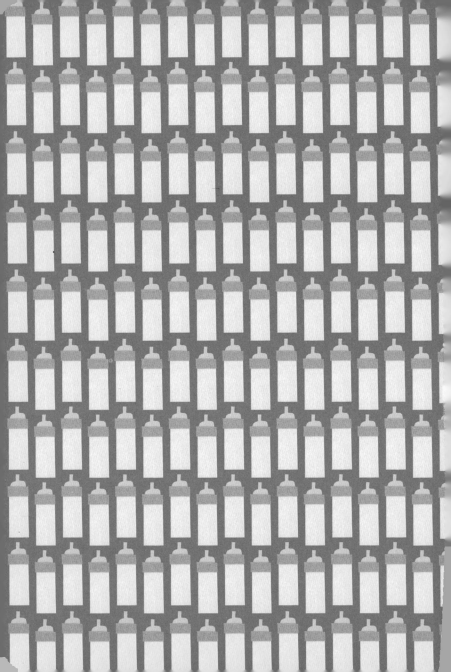

WELCOME TO THE CLUB

Welcome to the Club

100 PARENTING MILESTONES YOU NEVER SAW COMING

RAQUEL D'APICE

creator of The Ugly Volvo blog

CHRONICLE BOOKS

SAN FRANCISCO

Library of Congress Cataloging-in-Publication Data

Names: D'Apice, Raquel.
Title: Welcome to the club : 100 parenting milestones you never
saw coming /
  Raquel D'Apice.
Description: San Francisco : Chronicle Books, 2016.
Identifiers: LCCN 2015046632 | ISBN 9781452153476 (hardcover
: alk. paper)
Subjects: LCSH: Parenting—Humor.
Classification: LCC PN6231.P2 D38 2016 | DDC 649/.10207—
dc23 LC record available at http://lccn.loc.gov/2015046632

Manufactured in China

Designed by Tonje Vetleseter
Illustrations by Raquel D'Apice

10 9 8 7 6

Chronicle Books LLC
680 Second Street
San Francisco, California 94107
www.chroniclebooks.com

To my mother, my father,
and Titi, for somehow getting
me to adulthood.

And to Jonathan, for making
adulthood feel like the best
parts of childhood.

CONTENTS

Introduction   **8**

The Early Days   **13**

Oops   **29**

This Is Disgusting. Please Send
Reinforcements.   **41**

Interactions with Other Adults   **51**

Eating, Sleeping, and Other Total Disasters   **65**

Minor Panic Attacks   **79**

Toys, Games, and Other Vague Attempts
at Recreation   **95**

Stolen from the Traditional Baby Book   **107**

"It All Goes By So Fast!"   **117**

Stuff You Never Saw Coming   **129**

Acknowledgments   **142**

INTRODUCTION

I bought a baby book to record my son's milestones because I thought that was something I was supposed to do. The book had all the milestones I expected it to have. First tooth. First word. First step. Most of these books are the same. Sometimes they have "creative" prompts, tipping you off on what to write to your child.

The first time I saw your face _____

My favorite part of the day with you is _____

A cute thing you did recently was _____

And then there are the dates, which baby book manufacturers seem to feel are *very* important. *What was the date of his first car ride? Her first bath? His first visit to Nana's house?* After about 15 seconds of these I want to scrawl "I CANNOT BRING MYSELF TO CARE ABOUT ANY OF THIS" in block letters across the page. *Today he rolled from back to front* is not a story I would tell people over coffee unless I was hoping they would fall into a sleep deep enough for me to steal their iPhones or draw penises on their foreheads in Magic Marker.

Still, like everyone, there are days when I feel like completing these prompts with gushes of overpowering love.

The first time I saw your face, I held you with tears in my eyes, totally overwhelmed by your existence.

My favorite part of the day with you is when you sleep on my chest with your legs askew like a little tree frog.

A cute thing you did recently was blow kisses to the people in the waiting room of the dentist's office.

But those answers are not the entirety of the parenting experience. There are other answers that are just as valid as the ones above. Many days, when confronted with these sentences, my first instinct is to write:

The first time I saw your face, I felt like running away into the woods to avoid the responsibility of raising a child.

My favorite part of the day with you is the part where you are not screaming the words "PANTS OFF! PANTS OFF!" while also having a bowel movement in a restaurant.

A cute thing you did recently was eat a molted cicada skin in the parking lot of a Talbots.

While traditional baby books focus on recording *baby* milestones, this book is an attempt to highlight the *parenting* milestones all of us go through. Not to record them, per se, since we may not need a book with prompts like:

First time he sneezed into your mouth _____

or

Number of hours spent anxiously second-guessing all your decisions _____

Instead of a book of milestones you halfheartedly hope you'll remember, this is a book of occurrences you will probably never forget. It is a list of things that are happening to all new parents but which people are hesitant to talk about, lest they seem like they are doing a mediocre job.

This is not a book designed to be read all in one sitting, because the phase of your life when you could read things all in one sitting is (I'm sorry!) probably behind you. This book doesn't claim to have all (or possibly any) of the answers, but rather accepts that a lot of the time the answers will be different for each of us. It is a book to remind you that a lot of what you are going through is real and normal, even when it seems like it was staged by a special-effects department.

This is a book to let you know there will be different levels of hardships—some that you'll handle with a smile and a good-natured eye roll, and some that will make you sob hysterically into your phone because you want your old life back. It's okay. This book is a reminder that both of these things will pass and that, anxious as you may be about everything that is happening, you will somehow make it through all of this in one piece.*

Having a child is a new experience for everyone involved. Your child emerged from a quiet, fluid-filled sack into a world filled with angst, reality show spin-offs, and an overwhelming number of gum flavors. You emerged from your cocoon of childlessness into a world in which you spend hours trying to pull dried boogers out of someone's nose using plastic tweezers.** Being a parent is a marathon of unpredictable insanity. This book is an attempt to celebrate the chaos.

Welcome to the club.

*Probably.
**If you haven't done it yet, it's eerily similar to the Hasbro game Operation.

THE
EARLY
DAYS

1

First Time You Hold Your Child

Immediately after giving birth a nurse asked me, "Would you like to hold the baby?" and I said, "No," because I did not feel ready.

For some people, holding a baby is the most natural thing on earth, and for the rest of us it is only slightly less stressful than being asked to hold a grenade. For those of us regularly shattering our iPhone screens, the idea of being responsible for a delicate human life can be overwhelming because we are not sure we are cut out for the job. "Here," a nurse will say. "You know that tiny, miraculous human with a head like a Fabergé egg who means more to you than anything in the world? We'd like to place him in your arms, despite the fact that every fifteen minutes you trip over your laptop cord."

2

First Time Packing a Diaper Bag

I used to take pride in the fact that I could leave my house with nothing but my wallet, keys, and phone, and I can't wait to revisit that lifestyle at some point in my early seventies.

Babies need a lot of things and you'll never know which things they'll need at which times. If you're wondering, "How much stuff do I need to bring if I'm out with a baby for forty minutes?" the answer is "Only slightly less than someone traveling the Oregon Trail." A good rule of thumb is to bring everything you need to survive for 4 to 6 months in the wilderness for each hour spent outside the house.

First Baby Carrier Ride

1 Fasten child safely and snugly against your chest, adjusting the straps to be certain child is secure.

2 Walk out of house smiling. Congratulations! You are a real parent now, just like the parents pictured on the carrier packaging, only your hair has not been washed as recently.

3 Quickly check on baby to make sure baby is still breathing, because her face is buried in the fabric of the carrier and she could suffocate.

4 Assess that she is breathing and seems fine. Keep walking! People are looking at you and thinking, "How wholesome and tender! If I ever become a parent I would like to look as self-assured as that man/woman with the infectious smile and ineffable look of contentment!"

5 Check again on the breathing thing.

6 Shrug and go, "Oh, I am being so ridiculous! I need to lighten up. Obviously she is totally fine. People use these things every day!" Remind yourself that other primates, like lemurs and orangutans, carry their young in a similar manner with low suffocation rates.

7 Smile! Parenthood is very primal and fulfilling!

8 Wonder if lemurs are in fact primates???

9 Decide you should be supporting the carrier with both arms since you are not convinced you have secured it correctly. Realize that if you trip and fall you will land on baby.

10 Worry about this while simultaneously checking (again) to make sure baby is breathing. Are you still smiling? Keep smiling!

11 Ascertain that child is still breathing. (You think? How can you even really tell? Mirror test?)

12 Walk with one hand supporting baby and the other awkwardly extended to break your fall if you trip on something, looking not unlike a football player who is both cradling the ball and trying to avoid being tackled.

13 Walk one block before deciding that maybe this is not worth it and you should turn around and go back.

14 Arrive back home and frantically scan carrier instructions for any mention of babies suffocating in or falling out of or being crushed in carriers. Wonder if anxiety over this issue negates any joy derived from carrier use. Stare in dismay at the detailed diagram showing you how to put it on.

15 Google the Wikipedia entry for lemurs to ascertain that yes, they are, in fact, primates.

First Time You Try to Install a Car Seat and Curse Yourself for Not Getting That PhD in Theoretical Physics

Little-known fact: After his work on relativity was well received, Einstein presented the scientific community with instructions on how to correctly install a child's car seat, to which the scientific community responded by rubbing their heads and saying, "Stop! Stop! Too confusing!"

Baby's First Photo Session

Good newborn photographers must be exceptionally skilled, as most parents have incredibly high hopes for their photo shoot and most newborns look like Gollum from *Lord of the Rings*.* Much of a newborn photographer's job is to distract people from the fact that (while much beloved) your child looks like a cross between a naked mole rat and a miniature, shriveled version of your father-in-law. While some parents opt for a simple, JCPenney-style photo shoot, others bring in a professional photographer whose fees range from what you'd pay for a fancy dinner for two to the cost of a used car.

Newborns, in general, are not beautiful. But yours will be beautiful to you. Yours will be so beautiful that you will stare at her, dumbfounded, marveling at the tiny perfectness of her wrinkled legs. The real, actual job of a newborn photographer is to take photographs of your baby that (using soft lighting and a variety of cute, crocheted hats) will allow everyone else to see what you see.

Obviously not yours. Yours is adorable. But some of the others, right?

First Time You Realize That All the Thought You Put into Decorating the Nursery Was Not That Important

I have no experience in interior design (and until a few years ago still utilized milk crates as furniture), and yet I became strangely excited by the idea of decorating a nursery. A serene nursery where everything came together perfectly, like one I had seen once on a design website. Tasteful but inexpensive! Comforting enough for a baby (soft colors!) and yet engaging enough for a child (also bright colors!). I wanted a beautiful library corner with display shelves made from white vinyl rain gutters (Pinterest) and my child's name on the wall in fabric letters (Etsy), and I wanted a wooden rocking chair where I would sit endlessly with my child and indulge the insatiable love of reading he would obviously have. I sewed him a little blanket despite the fact that I had no idea how to sew, and found a beautiful watercolor print I decided to have custom-framed (which, for those of you who have never had anything custom-framed, is only slightly less expensive than buying a solid-gold yacht).

Did I enjoy decorating my nursery for my son's arrival? I did. That being said, setting up a beautiful, color-coordinated nursery for the arrival of a newborn is like putting on formal wear to walk through a hurricane.

7

First Time Breastfeeding the Baby

Breasts. You may know them as "things that make jumping rope difficult," and "the cause of Dolly Parton's inevitable back problems." Now a diminutive person you met only recently wants to drink fluid out of yours.

Questions you might have about this:

Q: Is the whole breastfeeding thing as magical as people say?

A: Okay, here's the thing. As weird as it sounds, yes—it can be. In the quiet sort of way where a thing you considered abhorrently bizarre brings you a strange sort of inner peace and connectedness to another person—yes, for some people it can be magical. In addition to being good for the baby, many women find that it is extremely rewarding and strengthens the bond between them and their children.

Q: Is it ever not magical?

A: Sometimes, for some people, it is not magical.

Q: Hey, uh, so just hypothetically, if it turned out I was one of the people for whom it is not magical . . .

A: Wait, you didn't find it magical??

Q: No! I mean I did! I mean I found it sort of magical . . .

A: (Gestures for other people to come over) Hey, everyone— look who didn't find breastfeeding magical!

Q: (Runs into dark alley to escape from angry villagers, many of whom are roaming the streets with medieval-style torches, looking for people at whom to hurl rocks)

Okay, we sort of lost our focus. Let's try this again on the following page.

Breastfeeding. Feeding out of the breasts. It seems as if women fall into three categories:

Women who managed to breastfeed exclusively

This is great. Are you doing this? You are a superhero. For real. Breastfeeding is really healthy for the baby. Yes, it is hard and tiring. Yes, sometimes you wake up with your body smelling like spoiled milk and it is gross, and sometimes there is something inside your breasts that feels like walnuts. (WHAT ARE THOSE?) Yes, sometimes you feel like a cow and PUMPING IS TERRIBLE, especially when you are also working, and yes, it is sometimes harder for a partner to help with feeding duties since the baby cannot drink the nectar of life out of the father's sagging pectoral muscles. But in general breastfeeding is wonderful. Did you do it? Fabulous job. Ten points to Gryffindor.

Women who were like, "I'm totally going to breastfeed," and who after a few weeks of breastfeeding were like, "Uh, f**k this."

"I'm definitely going to breastfeed," I thought. And then I attempted breastfeeding.

Part of it was that I never produced *anywhere close* to enough milk, while other women were packing their freezers like breast milk–collecting squirrels. Part of it was the back pain and the sensation that I was having my nipples chewed off by raccoons. And part of it was that no matter how much advice I got and no matter how many articles I read, nothing I did seemed to help or make any difference. Other mothers around me seemed to have visible rays of sunlight emanating from their faces, while I was constantly miserable and the baby was miserable and anyone who had to be around me was miserable.

So I stopped completely after about two months. And part of it, the main part of it, was that, much like a job in finance or a pair of madras capri pants, while it works fine for some people, it just didn't work for me. So my son drank formula. Which may not be as perfect for the baby as breast milk, but which was (at least in my case) much more plentiful. And rather than having a mother who was unhappy and constantly doubting herself and wondering what she was doing wrong, he had a mother who was upbeat and happy and not overwhelmed by self-doubt. I don't know if they've done any studies on that, but it must count for something.

Women who did not breastfeed or even attempt to breastfeed
So look—you really don't want to breastfeed? That's your decision. Do you love and care about your baby and are you doing the best you can with the resources you have? *Wonderful.* That is more or less the criteria for being a good parent. I never had breast milk as a child and I somehow made it to my mid-thirties without getting tuberculosis or murdering anyone.

First Outing with the Baby When You Forget Something Crucial

You decide to take your infant for a long walk in her stroller, and you are out with her, a mile from home, when she begins to cry. After a few dozen unsuccessful guesses you are able to deduce what she wants—her pacifier. No problem. You'll just reach into the diaper bag and grab her OMFG, YOU CANNOT

BE SERIOUS, WHERE IS HER *#%&ING PACIFIER?

For some reason (possibly because you never get more than three hours of uninterrupted sleep) you have forgotten to pack her pacifier. Here's what happens next.

1 A mass text message will be sent out to all parents in a two-mile radius, alerting them to the fact that you are such a terrible parent you somehow forgot to pack the one thing that comforts your daughter.

2 An enormous cartoon arrow will appear alongside you, pointing you out to anyone who was not on the list for the text message.

3 Nearby newspaper editors hankering for a juicy story will be contacted and will immediately begin typing the headline "Local Parent Unable to Handle Demands of Parenthood." The comments section of the eventual article will be a turf war of unconscionable hostility.

4 Your child will grow up cheerless and unable to experience joy. She will eventually drop out of school, fall in with the wrong crowd, and spend her life chasing an elusive happiness that will always seem just beyond her grasp.

I am kidding! Do you know what will happen? *Absolutely nothing.* Your child will cry for a while and you will eventually get home and give her the pacifier and she will be totally fine. On your walk home you will pass no fewer than four other parents with enormous cartoon arrows hovering next to their strollers and oh my god, don't stress about this.

9

First Time You Have the Thought "What If Having a Baby Was a Mistake?"

First and foremost, do not panic that you are a terrible person if you briefly think this. You are not.

Having this thought is terrifying.

I absolutely had this thought.

People who loudly insist that they have never had this thought and are aghast that anyone else would have this thought probably have this thought four or five times an hour.

Here is the thing. The thought "What if having a baby was a mistake?" is not really you thinking that having your child was an actual mistake. The thought "What if having a baby was a mistake" is your mind's way of asking, "What if I was not ready for this?"

And *of course you weren't ready for this. No one is ready for this.* I have met zero people who went into parenthood and were like, "Yes, of course, this is *exactly what I expected*!"

First Time You Feel Like You Love Your Baby

Some of you are reading this and saying, "*Wait, what does that even mean? You love your baby the first moment you see your baby. Sometimes you love your baby even before it is born. That's what happens to everybody, right?"* If you are one of those people, good news: you can step out for pizza for the entire next paragraph!

Hi! Are the rest of you still reading? Everybody get in close—cluster together so I don't have to say this next thing too loud. Okay, are you ready? Not everyone is going to feel like they love their baby right off the bat. I know we all feel like we are supposed to be hit with a parental tidal wave of love the moment the baby is placed in our arms, but when I was handed my son I felt more or less how I would have felt if someone had handed me a seven-pound bag of sweet potatoes.*

You may not feel like you love your baby right away. For some of you it will feel like you're on a date with a perfectly nice person who you feel like you should love but for whatever reason there's no chemistry. Sometimes the spark takes a while. I loved my son in that I did all the things for him you would do for someone you love. But I didn't feel what I thought I was supposed to feel. When people asked if I was totally head over heels in love with him, I would either lie and say yes, or (more often) comically cross my fingers and say, "Not yet, but any day now!" the way I respond when asked if the overalls-and-baggy-flannel-shirt look is making a comeback.

If we want to be really precise, I felt how I would have felt if someone had handed me a seven-pound bag of sweet potatoes that I had just pushed through my vagina during the most horrific, painful experience of my life, i.e., resentful of the sweet potatoes.

OOPS

First Time the Baby Accidentally Head-Butts You in the Lip (Or Nose. Or Eye Socket.)

It is amazing that a head that feels as fragile as an eggshell when you are cradling it in your hands inexplicably feels like a bowling ball when it is crashing into your face. At some point you will be holding your child and she will lose control of her neck and her head will come crashing into your face like a sledgehammer trying to destroy a building.

First Time Your Child Rolls Off the Bed/Sofa/Changing Table

Most scientists agree that the speed at which a child can go from being safely on the bed to being on the hardwood floor crying hysterically is so great, such children could (theoretically) escape the gravitational pull of a black hole.

Watching a baby on a bed is like being a security guard in an incredibly boring mall. You get hired and spend months being extremely vigilant, waiting to help avert disaster, and for week after week nothing happens. You show up every day in your security guard hat and jacket, ready to chase down someone stealing CDs, or whatever the heck kids are stealing nowadays. But nothing happens. And after a few months of this your brain goes, "Okay, I guess I don't have

to be as careful anymore," and instead of being vigilant 24/7, your brain starts thinking about something else, like what was the name of the bald actor who was in that Coen Brothers movie but is also in a commercial for some sort of insurance (J. K. Simmons), or how many calories are in a churro (116), or how on earth does anyone beat level 125 in Candy Crush (I HAVE NO IDEA), and whoa, hey, your kid's on the floor.

First Time You Foolishly Wear a
Top with an Elastic Neckline

Hi, everyone on the uptown 2 train. I bet you were wondering what my bra looked like. So happy I could help answer your question today. This model is $14.99 at T. J. Maxx. Nude underwire. Detachable crossback straps. I would've worn a nicer one if I had known everyone would be looking at it, but I momentarily forgot that my nine-month-old views me more as a rock climbing wall than as a human being who can experience anxiety and shame. Shout-out to the guy opposite me on the train frantically trying to concentrate on his newspaper.

First Time Your Child Hurts Himself
in a Room You Were Positive You Had
Sufficiently Childproofed

You bought all those little things for the outlets, right? And the little foam corners that go on the edges of tables and stuff? You got those? Great! Did you get the venetian blind cord thing and that C-shaped thing that keeps them from closing their fingers in the door? And the stove knob things? Did you move all your delicate or breakable stuff onto high shelves and put dangerous stuff like knives and matches well out of reach? Awesome, nice work. Did you put the gates up?

What about stuff like foam floor pads? Oh, hold up, did you install that thing where if he's toddling down the carpeted hallway and he trips over his own feet he won't fall and split his lip open on the monogrammed stepstool your parents bought him?

Children are magnets for disaster. I grew up in a house with soft carpeting and cabinet latches and baby gates, and yet one of my earliest memories is of picking up a popcorn kernel that had jumped out of the pot on the stove, even as my mother screamed, "NO, STOP, DON'T TOUCH IT!" and being initiated with a sizzling sound into the world of first-degree burns.

Your child is going to get hurt, even though sometimes the thought of this is paralyzing. Their fingers will get burned and their hands will get pinched in doors, and at some point probably their hearts will get broken. All the whale-shaped faucet covers in the world will not prevent this.

First Time the Baby Says a Word You Didn't Want Her to Say

Heads-up: Children are going to say things that are going to make you laugh and make other people laugh and that will also horrifically embarrass you. Sometimes she will say something because she heard you say it (i.e., all the curse words). Sometimes she'll say it because she can't pronounce something correctly (for example, "That elephant

wants some penis."*) Sometimes it'll happen because you felt the need to teach her the words for her genitals thinking that it's probably time she learned them, only to have your child approach every woman in your local Starbucks, gleefully announcing that they all have vaginas.

*You know. Penis. Like what George Washington Carver used to make soap. The thing to which my sister has a horrible allergy. Buy me some penis and Cracker Jack. Penis.

First Time You Spend Close to an Hour Getting the Baby Ready to Leave the House and a Half-Millisecond Getting Yourself Ready

I remember one day I had spent around forty minutes getting the baby ready to go outside, and as I prepared to carry the stroller down the stairs my husband said, "Diapers, wipes, bottle, burp cloths?" and I said, "Yep!" And he said, "Extra outfit, pacifier, sunscreen?" and I said, "Yep!" And he said, "Shoes?" and I assured him that yes, the baby was wearing shoes, and he said, "Yes, but you aren't."

I have (more than once) nearly left the house without shoes. On a regular basis I make it to 2 p.m. before realizing I have not eaten anything, at which point I begin frantically devouring my son's Goldfish crackers. I once made it as far as the park before realizing I still had dried Clearasil on my face.

First Time the Baby Hits the Buttons on Your Laptop and Irreversibly Deletes Something

If you put 100 chimpanzees at 100 typewriters and left them there for an infinite amount of time, eventually one of them would type out the entirety of the play *Hamlet*, and if you leave one young toddler at a computer keyboard for more than fifteen seconds, she will somehow download Adobe, delete a 730-page novel you were a week from finishing, and inexplicably upload a photo of Thomas the Tank Engine to your Facebook page.

Children and technology do not mix well. I feel fairly confident saying that the only people more bafflingly awful at using computers than your children are your parents.*

When I first started blogging, my mother enthusiastically told me she was "sharing my blog entries with everyone," which I later learned meant she was physically printing them out, stapling them into booklets, and handing them indiscriminately to the people in her office.

18

First Time You Make a Mental Note of Something Far Enough Away That She Definitely Can't Reach It and Two Seconds Later It Is Somehow in Her Hands

A child who wants to reach something is like a professional magician. "For my next trick I will effortlessly tip over a glass of wine twenty feet away while simultaneously grabbing a steak knife from this locked drawer."

"That's ridiculous," you're saying, with the smug face of a practiced skeptic. You are crossing your arms in front of your chest, daring the magician to make good on her promise. "She's little! She's strapped into her chair! There's no way she could get to that steak knife/knock over that glass/get out of her restraints/saw a woman in half."

And like many good magicians will tell you, magic is all about distraction. About focusing the audience's attention somewhere else long enough to make sure they're not looking too closely when you perform the trick. By the time your eyes are back on her, she is out of her restraints, the glass has been tipped, the knife has been grabbed, and (if you are extremely unlucky and she has been holding the steak knife for more than four seconds) something will have been sawed in half, and depending on what it was you should probably call either a carpenter or an ambulance.

First Time the Baby Totally Destroys Something of Yours

To get a feel for what life with a young child is like, watch some of the old Godzilla movies but in your mind's eye replace Tokyo with whatever your living room used to look like.

Envision your living room filled with hordes of people screaming. Frantically running. Godzilla enters, his claws immediately destroying the hardwood floors you had been hoping to maintain for when you resell the house. (RUN! EVERYONE GET OUT!) He roars and crashes unforgivingly into the glass media console *(Please, no, not the media console, that was a wedding present!)*, un-nesting the side tables and leaving the pendant lamp shattered in the entryway. The monster's cry echoes as he climbs the row of IKEA Hemnes bookcases, screeching and hurling copies of David Sedaris

books at cowering pedestrians, his fiery breath burning through both the dark gray tufted ottoman and the vintage Pendleton throw blanket that "tied the room together." (OH, THE HUMANITY!) Godzilla turns toward you, his path a chaos of fire and rubble. Your friends look on in horror, knowing there is nothing they can do to save you.

First Time You Forget to Lock the Wheels on Your Stroller

If there were an Olympic footrace where the only people competing were Carl Lewis, Usain Bolt, and me trying to catch a stroller that was rolling away, I would have landed a Nike endorsement deal before I even had time to hike up my high-waisted Lycra running pants. I do not understand why car manufacturers make such a big deal about their cars going zero to 60 in only a few seconds, when clearly stroller manufacturers have had that technology for decades.

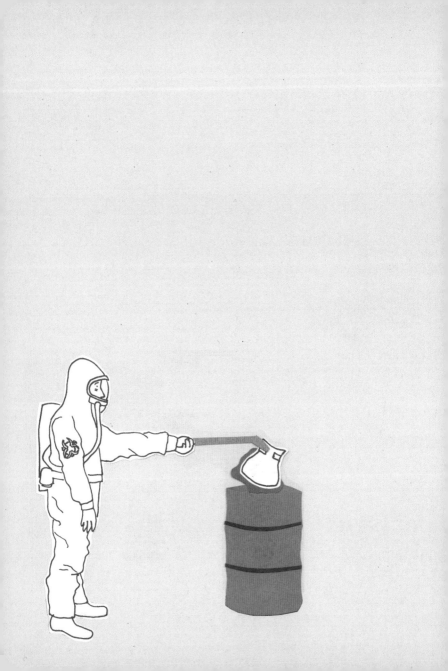

THIS IS
DISGUSTING.
PLEASE SEND
REINFORCE-
MENTS.

Baby's First Ungodly Poop Explosion

If we could harness the destructive power of children's bowel movements, the United States could easily cut military spending by a third. I don't want to brag, but one time after a stomach illness my son produced a fecal version of the *Game of Thrones*' "Red Wedding."

The amount of feces babies produce is both mind-blowing and humbling. I've seen excrement shoot up my son's back and neck like mercury in an old-fashioned thermometer. There will be items of clothing that you will, without a moment's hesitation, throw in the garbage, because the idea of their ever being clean again is laughable, and you'll have the thought, "Is everyone else using *this many wipes*?" as you tidy up something roughly as overwhelming as the Exxon Valdez oil spill.

Baby's First Poop Explosion Where She Reaches Down and Gets It on Her Hands

So you thought the poop explosion from the last paragraph was bad, and you're not wrong—it was. And yet the one factor that can make or break any pooping disaster is whether or not your child manages to get any of the poop on her hands. If your child's feces are a deadly tropical disease that is threatening all of humankind, your child's hands are patient zero.

Keep it off her hands and there is a chance that, disgusting as it is, it can be contained. Once it's on her hands know that it is also probably in her hair, her mouth, your hair, and then almost without warning on your hands, your clothes, the changing table, your neck, and probably the rug. Suddenly it is somehow in the living room and in the car and all over your mailman. Just when you think it can't spread any farther, you'll find traces of her bowel movement on your dog, aboard remote Antarctic research vessels, and in small Polynesian villages.

Do your best to keep disaster at bay. Godspeed.

23

Baby's First Constipation

Given how disgusting their poop is, you might assume it would be a relief when they're not pooping for a while. WRONG. They gave us a newborn baby and at one point he didn't poop for almost a week. And yes, for the first day or so a small part of me was going, "Gee, what a nice break from the foul-smelling fecal grenades he was detonating last Thursday," but very quickly the vast majority of me began to wonder what was wrong and how on earth he was going to pass something that seemed to be the size and consistency of a softball.

Helping a baby poop is rarely glamorous work. And as you are bicycle-pumping his legs or inserting glycerin suppositories into his rear end or lathering his tiny butthole with lubricant, it is natural for your mind to juxtapose what you are doing with whatever you considered the high point of your life. Like a former Oscar winner who is now starring in straight-to-DVD sequels, you will be going, "I was hailed as one of the most promising newcomers at a Fortune 500 company/led the management team of a major political campaign/won the National Book Award, and now here I am sticking gel caps into the anus of a sobbing eight-month-old."

The First Time You Get His Boogers All Over Your Hand and There Is Literally Nowhere to Wipe Them but on Your Clothes

A child's supply of boogers is as inexhaustible as the United States' supply of corn or Seattle's supply of rainwater or my mother's supply of advice on everything I'm doing wrong. Most of the time when your child's nose is running you will have a tissue or a burp cloth on hand. Sometimes you won't have a tissue or a burp cloth but you will have something else easily accessible—a piece of laundry that was already dirty or a small towel. Sometimes you will have something less than ideal but that still works (ATM receipt, absorbent piece of bread). And then occasionally, inexplicably, you will have nothing. You will reluctantly wipe their nose with your hand, after which you will wistfully wipe it onto the grass or on the sidewalk or, if it is just one of those days, on your beat-up running shoe or the cuff of your pants.

First Time Your Child Puts Her Mouth on Something So Disgusting You Debate Feeding Her Purell as a Meal

Some of the things babies put in their mouths are so revolting you are probably going to cringe a little when you read about them, and if I had my way and an unlimited amount of publishing money I'd put the following text under a lift-the-flap so you wouldn't have to see it if you didn't want to. Instead you have the option of either reading it or just knowing in general that children put really disgusting things into their mouths and moving on to the next page right now.

The answers from several parents on the grossest thing they have found in their child's mouth:

A wet pasta noodle from the floor of a shopping mall

The toilet brush (Hi, this one was me! I now have to keep my toilet brush on a hook mounted *near the ceiling* because my son regularly tried to grab it while I was showering.)

"We were in a public park, and I turned my back for a few seconds, and when I looked back at her she was eating pieces of chicken she found in a Styrofoam container behind a fence."

Dead insects—most notably stink and palmetto bugs (various parents)

Dog and cat food (various parents and also me)

Goose poop

Clumps of human hair from the shower drain

Another "I was in a public park and turned my back for a few seconds" story that ends with the child finding/attempting to eat a dead bird.*

*Okay, so the idea of your child even contemplating eating a dead bird is MIND-BLOWINGLY DISGUSTING, but the reason I included it was because whatever gross stuff your own child has accidentally put in his mouth, it is probably not as bad as a dead bird (good for you!), and on the off chance that your child has **also** gone after a dead bird, you should know you are not the only person who has had this happen (I had **three** parents give this answer). If your child has somehow gummed something **worse** than a dead bird, please e-mail me immediately as I desperately want to know what it was.*

First Time the Baby Resists Having His Diaper Changed

Q: I am trying to change my baby's diaper. Will he lie there happily while I do this like the babies in the commercials?
A: Hahahahahahahaha.

Changing a child who does not want to be changed is like trying to kidnap someone who refuses to stop break dancing. My son went through a phase in which he would flip his body over and over while I attempted to change his diaper, coating himself in feces the way you would bread a chicken cutlet. More than once if another person was in the room I would find myself saying something like *"Grab his legs! Hold down his legs!"* There are days when it will feel less like changing a baby and more like subduing an escaped prisoner.

27

First Time Her Diaper Rash Is So Bad You Decide to Leave the Diaper Off for a Bit to Let It "Air Out," and Within Five Minutes She Poops on the Floor

I remember someone telling me that the best way to cure diaper rash is just to let the baby walk around for a few hours without a diaper, and as long as you can cover every inch of your living room in clear plastic tarps and plastic wrap, it's a great idea you should totally try.

28

First Poop in the Bathtub

There are two kinds of these: the kind where lo and behold there is suddenly a Baby Ruth–size turd sitting politely beneath your son's rubber duck, and the kind where you hear gurgling and notice what seems like a hydrothermal vent in your child's bathtub and suddenly it looks as though you have been bathing her in a vat of pureed lentil soup.

I hope, for your sake, that it is the first kind.

First Time You Hold the Baby Over Your Head and He Vomits All Over You

Fun insider tip! In that scene from *The Lion King* where Rafiki is holding Simba aloft over his head, Simba is facing *away from Rafiki,* with his mouth directed outward, at the other animals gathered at Pride Rock. If you at some point feel the need to reenact this scene at home with your four-week-old, know that your cries of "*Naaaaaaaaaaaants ingonyama bagithi, Baba!*"* will be more moving if your child is not simultaneously vomiting into your mouth. Please learn from my mistake. You should no more hold a baby over your head than you should an open container of salad dressing.

Also, if you have a pressing need to know what the line means, the translation from Zulu is "Here comes a lion, father."

First Time You Pee Yourself

It's fairly well documented that this happens during pregnancy, but please know that many women will continue to regularly pee themselves even as their children enter college. Much to my dismay, I am no longer able to cough for long periods of time and/or jump rope. Here are some of the things you will attempt to do that will result in your peeing all over yourself.

Sneezing

Coughing too much

Laughing too much

Vigorous dancing

Not-particularly-vigorous dancing

"Going for a run" (read: a fast walk)

Eating a sandwich

Thinking about "going for a run"

Google-searching "Keep peeing in underpants post-pregnancy please help how make this stop???"

INTERACTIONS
WITH OTHER
ADULTS

The First Time You and Your Significant Other Either Fight or Quietly Resent Each Other Over Something Having to Do with the Baby

Having a baby is hard. Particularly for the first few months. You may feel angry and resentful a lot of the time because you feel like you are doing too much or your partner is not doing enough or your life has been turned upside down and you do not have any time for yourself anymore. That is normal. The first year of parenting can be brutal and you will need something to lighten the mood. To keep things upbeat, I've outlined some Fun Games to Play with Your Partner After the Birth of Your Baby.

Game #1: Pretending to Be Asleep!

It is 4:30 a.m. and the baby is crying hysterically. Despite the fact that a newborn is screaming in the adjoining room, you and your spouse pretend to be fast asleep! See who can keep up the charade for longer and which of you eventually breaks and goes to feed the baby. (Sucker!) On a scale from 1 to "could explode a building," try to measure the look the parent getting up shoots at the one who is still pretending to sleep.

Game #2: Points! Points! Points!

This is a super-fun one. For every grueling task you do concerning the baby, you are awarded a number of points. Changing a diaper. Taking her to the park so the other parent can take a shower. Taking her to the doctor.

Cleaning up a giant mess she made may be worth three points, while comforting her during a ninety-minute screaming fit may be worth ten. At the end of the day obsessively count up your points and angrily wave them in the face of your partner, who does not have as many points as you. Insist that you're supposed to have an even number of points. Go to bed feeling resentful. (Bonus!—Often this game can lead seamlessly into a round of Pretending to Be Asleep!)

Game #3: Imagination Vacation!
Go on a wild imaginative ride where you each think about the stuff you'd be doing if you *didn't* have a baby. Reading a book! Sleeping! Working at some sort of fulfilling job where you feel respected by other people! There is no end to where your imagination can take you! This game is best played in three-minute intervals while crying.

A quick note: You will probably play some of these games whether you want to or not. My husband and I have what I consider a really strong, wonderful relationship and we *still* found ourselves playing them. It will be hard, and I'm sorry. Practice saying, "I'm not angry at you and I'm not angry at the baby, I'm simply angry at this situation, which has robbed me of my free time, financial resources, autonomy, and sense of self." Good luck!

First Time a Stranger Gives You Aggressive, Unsolicited Advice on How to Raise Your Child

Having a child is like a Choose Your Own Adventure book, where you are constantly forced to make decisions with the added bonus that on every page there is some random person telling you his or her opinion about the adventure you chose.

You are in the clothing department of a Target and have a child who cannot yet walk but who desperately wants to move around. You are trying to hold him, but he is wriggling and wants to be put down. You cling to him but he fights you and starts to cry. You look at the floor. It is carpeted and there are not a ton of people around.

If you choose to put him down, turn to page 403.
If you choose to continue to hold him in your arms, turn to page 821.

Page 403: You put him down. He immediately stops crying and enthusiastically starts to move around. He crawls a bit and explores as you watch him carefully, making sure he doesn't get in anyone's way or put anything too gross into his mouth. Within moments a random woman approaches and tells you that that's disgusting, you can't have your child on the floor in a Target.

*Page 821: You continue to hold him and he continues to struggle. His cries become louder as you desperately try to both attend to him and find pants that fit you because you do not currently own any. He lets out an ungodly wail and you become acutely aware that you are that person with a **hysterically** crying baby in a Target. The same woman who approached you on page 403 walks by and shoots you a snide glance that says "It's pathetic that some people don't know how to manage their children."*

First Time You Have to Spell Something Out So the Baby Doesn't Realize What You're Talking About

Actual conversation I had with a man on the subway:

Man on Train: What a sweet kid! He's so verbal and aware of stuff for someone his age!

Me: I know, it's crazy! I'm at the point where I can't even say the C-word in front of him anymore!

Man on Train: (Silently averts his eyes from my face while his own face turns a bright, uncomfortable shade of crimson.)

Me: (suddenly realizing) OH MY GOD, *COOKIE, I MEANT COOKIE.*

First Date When You Try Desperately to Not Spend the Entire Date Talking About the Baby

You are going to do this cute thing at the beginning of the date where you go, "You look so nice," to your significant other, and he or she is going to say the same thing to you. And you are going to pretend it's one of those dates you had when you first met, where you were dressed up and falling in love with a stranger and excitedly talking about all the stuff people who don't have a baby talk about on dates. One of you will go, "So, uh, how was work?" and the other one will say, "It was good!" and then go, "Hey, did you see the video of that puppy falling asleep on that kitten/read about that politician in that crazy sex scandal/take that online quiz that tells you which Hogwarts House matches your personality?"* And the other person will go, "Yes! That was crazy!" and then there's going to be an awkward twenty seconds of silence in which both of you busily look for the waiter to take your order.

Usually within the first ten minutes one of you will break and say something like, "I know we're not talking about the baby, but she was so cute today, I have to show you . . ." and will pull out a video on his or her phone and the other one will scoot in excitedly to see it, and the waiter will look at you with pity and disgust because oh my god, what is wrong with this couple, they get one night out away from the baby and here they are, huddled gleefully over their phones, watching a video of a three-month-old burping like it's an HBO original series.

Ravenclaw, but I kept taking it until I got Gryffindor.

First Time You Foolishly Attempt to Have a Focused, Interesting Conversation with Another Adult While You Are Also Watching the Baby

Watching a baby, even a good-natured baby, is a full-time job. Sometimes you will forget this, or a kind friend will want to meet up and will say, "Just bring the baby with you!" which you can do, of course. But if you are hoping to have a deep, meaningful conversation with your friend, be aware that if the baby is with you, the conversation will be interrupted every fifteen seconds because the baby has wandered off or wants attention or is crying or has wandered off a second time or wants attention again or has broken something or is eating a dead bird.

It is easy to forget how much attention young children constantly require. It is important to remember that a baby is not a jazz musician who is softly playing in the background of your existence. A baby is a stand-up comic, aggressively asking you questions because you are sitting in the front row with a bad haircut. Adjust your expectations accordingly.

36

The First Time You Shyly Approach Another Parent to Ask if They Want to, You Know . . . Exchange Phone Numbers or Hang Out Sometime?

Now that you have children, you are going to need to befriend other people who have children. (Sorry, that is the rule.) This is often awkward, as most likely you have not had to "make friends" with total strangers since you were a teenager. Here are some of the ways to do this.

1 Attend a local mom's/dad's group. Find another parent whose parenting style seems sort of similar to your own and who seems sort of interesting (i.e., this person likes some of the TV shows you like and responds favorably to whatever movie quotes you are incessantly repeating). Pass them the below note:

Hi! I am a former <u>Name of Former Job Title at Name of Former Company</u> *who is now trapped in an apartment with a(n)* <u>Age of Child in Months</u>*-month-old who cannot speak. I like you. Do you like me back? Check one:*

☐ *Yes, I like you, too. Let's meet up over coffee and complain about sleep training and our area's questionable public schools.*

☐ *No, you seem weird.*

2 Take out a personal ad that reads: "Isolated parent of young child ISO same. Good conversationalist preferred. Must be okay with my breaking into tears at random intervals."

3 Stand outside a Gymboree like one of those people trying to raise money for charities and approach strangers with the phrase "Hi, may I have a minute of your time to save housebound adults from crippling loneliness?" while making an aggressive amount of eye contact.

First Time a Like-Minded Parent Friend Moves Away and You're As Sad As You Were When You Were Eight and Your Best Friend Moved Across the Country

You finally meet someone really cool and fun who has a kid your child's age. Have you found this person yet? Find them. It will feel, sometimes, like you have made a best friend at camp. Now you and this person will see each other all the time. Playdates. Meetups at the park. You will always look forward to seeing this person and each of you will hope/be positive that your children will eventually be best friends and/or possibly marry each other. Parenthood is hard, but suddenly it seems bearable now that this person is around.

Surprise! This person has to move because her job or her spouse's job requires her to relocate to a small village in Indonesia or a town in Kentucky with no Internet access. And what you will say is "Oh no! I can't believe you are leaving! (My child's name) is going to be so sad when (your child's name) leaves!" But that is not true. Your child is really young and will forget about the other child after a few months, if not right away. But YOU will be sad. Because your friend left.

First Time You Have Something Resembling a Romantic Relationship Again

If you met your spouse through an online dating site in which she listed her turn-ons as *"being exhausted"* and *"repeatedly reading* Go, Dog, Go," then lucky you, you are going to get right back into your sex life post-baby, no problem! If you find a woman who says that nothing puts her in the mood like twenty minutes of passive-aggressive dishwasher unloading, *marry her immediately, the sex will be amazing forever.*

Having a sex life is harder after the baby, but you can work on it. You will both be tired *a lot.* You will sometimes be sort of in the mood, and then right at that moment one of you will step on an electronic toy that begins enthusiastically counting to ten in Spanish and the mood will be killed in fewer than *uno dos tres* seconds.

Be patient. Help each other out as much as humanly possible. You will have a relationship again, even if occasionally that means having sex while absentmindedly thinking about preschool early enrollment *(should we have started looking into this??)* or your child's next round of vaccinations. The best thing you can do for your sex life (as boring and unromantic as this sounds) is to genuinely care about each other.

Baby's First Meetup with Another Baby That You're Really Excited About and Which Is Inevitably Cancelled

Finally! After what seems like eons of being cooped up alone with a baby, you are getting together with other parents and children. You will be overjoyed. Which is why it will be so heart-breaking when a playdate is cancelled. (And it will probably be cancelled.) Here are the reasons why it may not work out.

The other baby usually naps earlier, but today was weird and now he or she will be napping right when you were supposed to meet.

Your baby is napping.

The other baby seems like he or she is getting a fever.

The other baby has a fever.

The other baby is just getting over having a fever.

The other parent has a fever because for the past week he/she has been taking care of a baby with a fever.

The other baby is vomiting and the other parent is worried it might be serious.

Your baby has a fever, is getting a fever, is getting over a fever, or is vomiting.

You have a fever.

The weather is terrible and you will not be able to get to the place where you are supposed to meet up.

The other parent made a mistake and they're not free at that time (they are so sorry!).

You made a mistake and you're not free at that time (you are so sorry!).

The other parent is suddenly called into work unexpectedly.

The plans fall through due to a glitch in the time/space continuum.

A giant asteroid obliterates 70 percent of all life on earth.*

*Possibly you can reschedule??

First Time You Post a Photo of the Baby to Facebook and It Gets More Likes Than Anything You've Ever Done

The desire to show photos of your child to people will be almost as strong as the biological urge to have children in the first place. I cannot state this strongly enough. You may have previously browsed social media, thinking, "Gosh, so-and-so certainly posts a lot of photos of her baby," only to now find yourself choosing Instagram filters at 3 a.m. with the pulsating need of a heroin addict, uploading photo after photo while muttering, "Just a few more . . ."

You will get more Facebook likes on a cute photo of your baby than you would get if you posted a photo of yourself being sworn in to the Senate.* People you do not even remember friending on Facebook will emerge from the sewer tunnels in which they live to click "Like" or to comment "OMG, so precious!" before descending back into the mildew-filled underworld to eat rat corpses.

*A photo of a cute baby being sworn in to the Senate would possibly break the Internet.

EATING,
SLEEPING, AND
OTHER TOTAL
DISASTERS

41

First Time the Sleeping Technique That Some Book Promised Would Solve All of His Sleeping Problems Doesn't Solve Any of His Sleeping Problems

"Wow, so many mothers have trouble getting their children to sleep through the night successfully. Too bad none of them read that article I found online a few months ago that explains the right way to do it." —Me, right before having a baby

Have you ever had the hiccups and suddenly every Person in a twenty-foot radius would like to share their hiccup-cessation techniques with you? This one lady wearing too much vanilla body spray is telling you to breathe into this brown paper bag for a few minutes and then this other random woman keeps going, "Have you tried drinking water upside down?" and that's when some idiot you barely know jumps out and yells, "AAARRGHHH!" These people, believe it or not, are trying to help. Because the thing each of them is suggesting *really did work for their own hiccups,* and they are so excited to share their successful hiccup-stopping techniques with you.

You will read a lot about getting your child to sleep through the night—much of it in tired Google searches done on your phone at 2 a.m. You are probably going to try a sleep technique (which you are so positive will work!) that is not going to work. That is okay. Just try something else. If that doesn't work, try something else. Don't beat yourself up if someone else insists that the first technique worked great for them. Different things work for different kids.

42

First Time the Baby Sleeps a Little Longer Than She Normally Sleeps and You Immediately Freak Out

Your child has been sleeping for two hours at a stretch and so that is how you are sleeping as well. Two hours. Two hours. Two hours. And all you want out of life at this point is for the baby to sleep three or (do you dare to hope?) four hours at a stretch so you are not so tired that you almost brush your teeth with your spouse's eczema medication.* You fall asleep, accepting of but frustrated by the fact that you will be woken up in two hours.

And then suddenly you wake up. You wake up naturally—not because anyone is crying—and you are filled with a momentary serenity, followed by the sort of immediate anxiety you have when your alarm clock does not go off and you have an important meeting and you are late. You glance in the direction of the co-sleeper or the nursery or the bassinette in the hallway and realize that the baby is still asleep. And a small part of you will go, "Finally! He slept for five entire hours! Let me lie back in bed and enjoy this small moment of parenting bliss." But then another part of you, the part that is very well-meaning but is occasionally prone to bouts of fear-induced self-sabotage, says, "There is a 98 percent chance the baby has finally begun to sleep for longer periods, but there is a

*Happened once. Both things come in a similarly sized tube. Also, at the height of my sleep deprivation, I stepped onto an escalator and stood on it for almost fifteen seconds before I noticed it wasn't moving because it wasn't an escalator, it was just a regular staircase.

2 percent chance that something is wrong, and because of that 2 percent chance, let me now stand over my child's crib and obsessively watch to be sure he is breathing, inevitably waking him up with my presence." You wake him up and the child begins to cry, and while you are (as always) dismayed at the crying, you are so overwhelmingly relieved that he is okay. You are once again awake with a screaming infant, and yet everything feels right with the world.

First Time Your Baby Sleeps Through the Night

So for some people this happens at two months and for some people it happens after two years, but regardless of when it occurs, the first night your baby sleeps through the night you are going to feel sort of like those people standing on their front porches next to an enormous Publisher's Clearing House check. Is this really happening to you? It can't be. Oh my god, IS THIS REALLY HAPPENING? HOLD UP. OH MY GOD. I HAD HEARD FROM OTHER PEOPLE THERE WAS A CHANCE THIS COULD HAPPEN AND I CANNOT BELIEVE IT, THIS IS HAPPENING FOR REAL!! OMG, OMG, I HAVE TO TEXT LITERALLY EVERYONE I HAVE EVER MET. And some guy with a microphone is asking, "So how do you feel? Any idea how you're going to use all this newfound energy and free time?" and you're grinning from ear to ear, at a complete loss for words because you cannot believe this is REALLY HAPPENING TO YOU! YOU WON! YOU WON! YOU WON! CONGRATULATIONS!!

First Time Someone Gives You a Hard Time Because You Are Breastfeeding in Public

If you are breastfeeding, probably at some point you will have to breastfeed the baby in public, and if you do this there is a chance that someone will casually say that whipping out your breast like that makes them uncomfortable and they shouldn't have to look at it.

Let them know that they are right, they *should not have to,* which is why (get ready for some big news) human eyes have been equipped with small folds of mucus membrane–lined skin that (get this) *come down over the eyeball, temporarily blocking vision.* And if they get upset because it's not like they're going to walk around with their eyes closed, they will be excited to learn that *the eyeballs themselves can be moved in various directions* (as can the neck) in order to avoid looking at a stressful or unsavory stimulus. What a day, yes? *The human body is a miracle!*

I am not saying everyone around you will immediately be comfortable with your breastfeeding. You cannot control what other people will think or do. I guarantee that not everyone will think, "Such a beautiful example of maternal bonding!" because some of them will be thinking, *"Yipes, a nipple the size of an alarm clock!"* People think what they think. But what other people think is their own issue and you shouldn't have to breastfeed in a Taco Bell bathroom stall because of it.

First Time Someone Gives You a Hard Time Because You Are Feeding the Baby Formula

For a lot of my son's infancy I gave him formula and twice I had total strangers approach me and tell me that I was feeding my baby poison. They literally used the word "poison," as if the side of the formula container read as follows:

Ingredients in Formula: Organic Nonfat Milk, Drain Cleaner, White-Out Correction Fluid, Cyanide, Hemlock, Unfiltered Tap Water from That Town Where They Filmed Erin Brockovich, *Liquid Nitrogen, Battery Acid, Deadly Nightshade*

Both strangers had looked at me as if I were scum and for a brief moment, because I was so new to parenting and prone to second-guessing myself, I thought, "Maybe I *am* scum? Maybe they're right and I am as terrible as they think?" And in case this happens to you, know that no, you are not scum. You are fine.

I love my son so, so much. I am trying hard to be both a good mother and a good person, but often this entails making decisions that other people will not agree with. Sometimes there is nothing I can do to change people's minds about me, so I have to politely say, "Thank you so much for your opinion." And then go home and vent my frustration by drawing a picture of us in which I look very beautiful and kind and in which they look like the terrifying aunts from *James and the Giant Peach.*

First Time Your Child Refuses to Eat Something

Before your child eats solids, you're going to say, "What are other people talking about? If their children are refusing to eat something maybe it's *they* who are doing something wrong."

A year later, when your own child hits this stage you're going to wonder if maybe you could open her mouth using that Jaws of Life thing they use to get people out of burning, collapsed buildings or mangled cars. In general it is easier for a camel to pass through the eye of a needle than for broccoli to pass through the mouth of a two-year-old.*

*Also, most two-year-olds would happily let a camel walk through their mouth before they'd let the broccoli thing happen. Which is what makes it so frustrating. They'll go, "Sure, I'll eat this cigarette butt off the floor of a public bus, but don't expect me to eat this meal you've been preparing for the past two hours."

First Time the Baby Eats Dog or Cat Food

He didn't eat any of the mashed lentils you attempted to feed him an hour ago. You regularly leave a dish full of food *on the floor.* How did you think that was going to end?

First Time Taking Your Child to a Restaurant

If you go to a restaurant and your child has a breakdown, all eyes will be on you because *how could you be so inconsiderate as to take a child to a restaurant?* If you put your child in front of an iPad all eyes will be on you *because how could you be so uninvolved as to put your child in front of an iPad?* If you pay attention to and entertain your child the entire time all eyes will be on you because *if you go out of your way to entertain your child how will she ever learn how to entertain herself?* If you don't take her to a restaurant all eyes will be on you because *how on earth will she get used to behaving well in public if you don't give her the opportunity to learn by taking her to a restaurant?* HAVE FUN TRYING TO WIN. YOU WILL NEVER WIN.

That being said, here is some actual advice about bringing your child to a restaurant.

Start off taking your child to early dinners at 4 p.m. or so to see how she handles restaurants. If she does well, great. If she does

terribly, at least you know that, and the only people you've bothered are the people who go to dinner at 4 p.m.—i.e., my parents.

Do not let your child walk around a restaurant. Yes, they want to get down and move around, but a restaurant has dozens of people walking around carrying hot items and heavy ceramic dishes. It is the worst possible place to let a child walk. If they are fidgety, take them outside.

If they have a breakdown, take them outside to handle it.

Tip well. I try to give 20 percent minimum, as long as my server is doing his or her best. If you think being a parent can be a thankless job, try waiting tables.

First Complete Emotional Breakdown (Yours)

If you think a shirt from Forever 21 falls apart quickly, wait until you see how fast an adult human being can unravel.

I'm obviously not saying you're going to literally unravel, because you're fine, right? She can be a little trying at times, yes, but you are an adult and you can handle stressful situations without breaking into tears or lashing out at someone so small they need to stand on their tiptoes to reach a doorknob. The hysterical crying barely even bothers you. You're an adult and you know not to lose it even when she keeps hitting the dog and screaming and you're using your most calm, even voice and going, "What did we say about hitting Meatball? We have to be gennnntle with Meatball." And her voice is shattering the mason jars you use as drinking glasses and she is literally throwing herself into the rug like a football spiking itself into the end zone. But you are *fine fine fine* because you remember reading something about how you just have to let it pass and not engage with her, *which would just be so much easier if you knew why she was screaming— will somebody please explain why she is screaming? The sort of screaming that causes storm clouds to roll in and ocean waves to churn, and suddenly there is a Channel 11 news van and a reporter in a windbreaker telling people to please, for the love of God, stay in their homes. Somebody please help me, why is she screaming, if I can find a plate-glass window that her shrieks haven't shattered I'm going to put my head through it in the next seven seconds.*

50

First Time Flying with a Baby

Everyone is always very nervous at the idea of flying with a young child, but in reality it's no more stressful than swimming in a tank of bloodthirsty hammerhead sharks, and oh wow, did I write that? I'm *so* sorry, no no no, let me try again.

Okay, take two! I know you are nervous about this, but flying with a baby can actually be as relaxing as being chased through an abandoned cafeteria by a man wielding a staple gun and WHOA, SERIOUSLY, IS THAT WHAT I JUST TYPED? Sorry sorry sorry! Arrghhhh! It's like I'm trying to type the one thing about how flying with a baby is actually lovely and ~~not relaxing~~ relaxing and how you'll probably ~~have a better time setting your hair on fire~~ really enjoy it, and this computer keeps twisting my words around to make it sound like having a baby is going to be *TOTALLY HORRIBLE! SAVE YOURSELF, RUN RUN RUN FOR THE HILLS.**

*So now that you've read this and are on edge at the idea of ever having to fly with a baby, I will confess that I've flown with a baby. Multiple times. Is it fun? No, it is not fun. Was it relaxing? No, it was not relaxing. Was it filled with a mix of hard and beautiful moments ranging from having our child cry hysterically when the plane suddenly dropped altitude (I also cried at this) to having him sleep quietly on our chests for most of a seven-hour flight? Was it filled with both angry people who looked at us disapprovingly and amazingly kind people who made funny faces and asked if they could hold him and a lovely couple in Atlanta who randomly treated us to lunch during our layover? Absolutely it was all these things. Are most of my memories of flying with a baby good memories? They are. Do I still dread flying with him every time I have to do it? I do.

MINOR

PANIC

ATTACKS

51

First Time Your Child Bleeds While You're Trying to Cut Her Nails

You will notice your baby's nails at two times.

1 When you are gazing down at her hands, drunk on the nonsensical happiness of how small they are. (*Having ovaries + extremely small versions of regular-size things = elation. Explain??*)

2 When she wakes up from a nap with scratches on her face and you realize that her nails are wolverine-length and need to be trimmed.

The nails of a newborn are extremely small and extremely difficult to see. (Many brands of baby nail clippers have little magnifying glasses attached to them.) Also, bear in mind that the skin underneath the fingernails is one of the most pain-sensitive areas on the body. (People used to torture prisoners by placing splinters underneath their fingernails and then setting the splinters on fire. Have fun sharing that fact with people at parties!*)

So here is what will probably happen at some point. You will be cautiously holding the nail clipper and while clipping her nails you will cut her skin and she will cry and bleed a little. If you have not yet done this and are curious about how you will feel—it feels more or less the same as stabbing a letter opener into your own heart. Do you remember that scene in *The DaVinci Code*** where the old guy is flogging himself with some torture device because he feels like he is so terrible he needs to experience pain? Well, get ready, because you're finally going to understand him. The moment I saw a tiny red drop of blood on my son's fingertip I expected social services to burst through my wall like the Kool-Aid Man.

Don't beat yourself up. This happens to a lot of people. Also, invest in a nail file.

I'm kidding! You have a kid now! You will no longer be able to attend parties!
**Don't pretend you didn't read it. Everybody read it.*

First Time Leaving Your Baby with a Babysitter

Hello! Thank you so much for watching little [Insert Baby's Name Here] while we are out eating a hurried-yet-romantic dinner/seeing a movie for the first time in months/attempting to enjoy some higher form of "culture" while checking our phones every fourteen seconds to see if there are any messages from you. [Insert Baby's Name Here] is almost always happy and relaxed and should give you almost no problems, but just in case we have given you detailed notes to ensure that things go smoothly!

[Insert Baby's Name Here] usually goes to bed without a problem, as long as her bedtime routine is executed flawlessly and without variation.

6:00–7:34 **Dinner.** It's very important to us that she gets a good serving of fruits and vegetables! In the fridge is a container of organic, homemade zucchini quinoa and ricotta fritters. Cut two of them up into small (pea-size or smaller) pieces, mix with brown rice, and allow her to sprinkle it on the floor before giving her Cheerios or a mozzarella stick. If she clamors for a cookie, she is not allowed to have one unless she has eaten one-eighth of a fourth of the mozzarella stick. We are super strict about this!!

7:34–7:48 Bathtime. Bath toys are in a mesh bag under the sink. She is super great about bathing but, FYI, doesn't like having water touch her skin, so please be mindful!

7:48–8:00 She will want to sit in the rocking chair while listening to the Eagles (Note: NOT "HOTEL CALIFORNIA"). She'll be most comfortable if you sing along with most of the songs. If you don't know the lyrics, the three-ring binder with typed-out Eagles lyrics is on the bottom left-hand corner of the bookshelf.

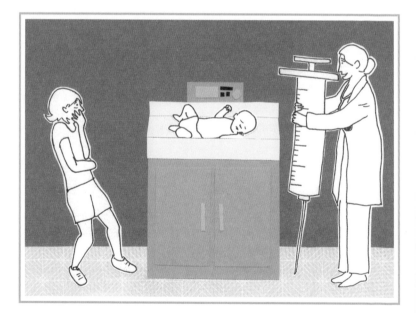

8:00-8:37 Read her *The Very Hungry Caterpillar* over and over, but skip the pages where the caterpillar is eating things other than fruits and vegetables. (Don't want to set a bad precedent!)

8:37-8:39 Change her diaper and either brush her teeth or casually forget to do this.

8:40-?? Rock her in the rocking chair with the lights off. If at any point she seems anxious or confused or indifferent please text me so I can incessantly worry about it! Thx!

First Doctor's Visit Where the Baby Has to Get Shots

"You know that tiny innocent being who fills your heart with joy? Would it be possible for you to pin his body to the table in this fluorescently lit windowless office so we can take something that looks like a long, unfolded paper clip and stick it into the tender skin of his thigh as his heart-wrenching screams echo through the hallway?"

Baby's First Time Getting Eyedrops or Ear Drops

So your child has been prescribed either eyedrops or ear drops. Seems pretty innocuous, right? If you want to know what this will be like:

Find some movie in which a shrieking, hysterical person is being burned at the stake.

Remove any traces of fire or smoke from the film using some sort of video-editing software so the subject is just tied to a pole screaming.

Use CGI to add in an additional person—this one calmly holding a bottle of either ear drops or eyedrops.

First Time the Baby Is Screaming Like She's Being Dipped in Sulfuric Acid but Nothing Seems to Be Wrong

Your child is screaming in her room and based on the pitch and volume and length of her screams your best guess is that she has either just witnessed a murder, is the protagonist in a horror movie, or is on fire. So imagine your confusion when you walk into the room to find—nothing. There is no villain in a hockey mask surrounded by panicked teenagers and there is no crime-scene tape being unfurled to the sound of the *Law & Order* theme song and there is no inferno of flame engulfing her copy of *Harold and the Purple Crayon. So why is she screaming?*

You pick her up. She doesn't seem to have a fever, nor is she tugging at her ear.* She isn't vomiting. She is simply screaming as if she has realized the futility of existence and could think of no quieter way to express her displeasure. She is screaming as if her voice could fill the whole of her existential emptiness—as if she has touched and is shouldering the pain of all mankind. And then, suddenly, her body will shift a little bit and you will hear a loud thwapping noise like a kazoo being played inside a horrifically soggy deli sandwich. And she will stop crying and will suddenly be totally fine because, surprise, it was just gas.

*An indication that she either has an ear infection or is about to steal third base.

First Time You Are Completely Overwhelmed by Loneliness

Parenting is lonely. I did not know this going in. There were days when being home alone with a baby felt like—you know that moment in a game of hide-and-seek when you realize that no one is looking for you? Like that, but lonelier.

Expecting a child is exciting. People are congratulating you and sending you gifts. There is a whimsical themed baby shower in your honor and relatives and friends are hugging you and taking pictures and sending you advice and love. And then, as if this has been an extravagant bon voyage party, the boat pushes away from the dock and you are standing on the deck all alone, holding this small confusing baby. And for a while you can still see everyone on the shore wishing you well and shouting, and the cannons shooting confetti and streamers up into the air. But after a while you see no one. There is just you. And the baby. Day in and day out. Some days things go well and other days, not so much. And you look out your

little porthole window and everything looks the same as it did the day before. It can be really boring.

AND YET, just out of sight past the horizon line is another ship with another parent holding a new baby. Who feels as lonely as you feel. And past that parent's horizon line there is another one. You cannot always see each other, but you are all going through the same thing at the same time. Find other new parents and reach out to them.*

A fun place to reach out is Facebook at 3 a.m., as the people logged on are either other parents restlessly rocking their infants back to sleep or incredibly drunk people. Messaging either will make for an interesting conversation!

First Time You Meet a Kid Your Child's Age Who Is Way More Advanced Than Your Child

People will frequently go out of their way to tell you how intelligent or literate or developmentally advanced their own children are. It can be maddening. The next time someone starts telling me how smart their child is, I'm going to say, "Oh, thank goodness your four-month-old is here—I was worried I'd go all day without meeting anyone who could solve the energy crisis!"

My son didn't take his first steps until he was 18 months old, at which point other 18-month-olds were choreographing elaborate tap dances. It's fine. Some children recognize the inherent absurdity in David Foster Wallace's *Infinite Jest* before other children recognize their own hands. Don't start frantically worrying if your child isn't exactly where you think he should be.

First Time You (Briefly) Lose Track of Your Child in a Playground or Supermarket

You know the panic you've felt when you have somehow lost a really important document on your computer? Where you're going no, this can't be happening, you couldn't have lost the document you've been working on *night and day for almost two years,* it must be backed up somewhere. You must've remembered to save all the changes or e-mail it to yourself because YOU COULD NOT HAVE LOST THAT DOC-UMENT. Okay, so take that panic and multiply it by a million billion trillion. Now take that new number and multiply it by the number of hydrogen atoms in the sun and then multiply THAT number by five. Write the final number on a piece of paper and then set the paper on fire and then drop the flaming pieces of paper into your eyes.

Your son is meandering through the playground, toddling amongst other babies and broken pieces of chalk. The mother of one of the other children asks the age of your son and you say, "Around fourteen months," and she smiles and says yes, hers, too. She asks if you used to go to that meetup at the coffeehouse on Wednesdays and you say yes, and if you are wondering if all conversations at playgrounds are this boring, yes, a lot of the time they are, it is nobody's fault. You glance over at your son but suddenly he isn't where he was a second ago. And you smile at the other mother and go, "Hold on one second," and she nods and you jog around the playground because probably he is over by the bench, just out of your sight. But he isn't there. And your heart tightens up a little, but you assume he must've walked back toward the slides. But you check and he isn't there, either. And as you start to panic you tell yourself, "Don't panic, it's a fenced-in playground, he's obviously here somewhere." You walk a full lap around the playground looking at every kid and you do not see yours. Suddenly you are rocking back and forth, gasping for air like Uma Thurman in *Pulp Fiction* right after they stab her with a shot of adrenaline in the heart, because oh my god, where is he? YOU COULD NOT HAVE LOST HIM. HOW COULD YOU HAVE SPENT FOUR SECONDS TALKING WITH ANOTHER PARENT WHEN YOU SHOULD HAVE BEEN LOOKING AT HIM AT ALL TIMES—HOW COULD YOU HAVE TAKEN YOUR EYES OFF HIM?

And as an invisible hand ruthlessly squeezes the blood from your heart, you hear the voice of another mother say, "Hey, he's over here, he sat down in our stroller to watch the squirrels." And you walk over to the other woman and there is your son, happily nestled into some lady's umbrella stroller watching a squirrel run across the top of the fence. And because it would be weird to burst into tears in the middle of a public playground, you grin and go, "Whoa, got nervous there for a second!!" And the other mother goes, "Totally! Kids, right?" And you both smile and laugh about it and forty minutes later you go home, where you collapse into a sobbing pile of wild, unrepressed anguish.

First Time You Drop Off Your Child at Day Care and Second-Guess Everything About Your Life

You are dropping off your child at day care so that you can rejoin the workforce. As difficult as it is, part of you feels wonderful and fulfilled because after spending months in a vomit-stained crewneck T-shirt, you will finally have a reason to wear clothes that require ironing and be able to interact with the type of person who, when handed a business card, doesn't immediately put it in her mouth.

You hold your daughter to your chest and kiss her good-bye, and that is when she lets out a cry, which, if interpreted by a UN translator, would read: "Please don't walk away from me. Your leaving me here will sabotage any chance of my being able to connect with other people in a meaningful way."

Leaving a crying child can hurt. It is hard to explain how much it can hurt. Remember the story of the Sirens from *The Odyssey*, where, if you heard their cries, you'd find yourself wildly, irrationally drawn to them? That is how it will feel. You will hear your daughter and your heart will literally *ache* to go to her, even while on many levels you will be desperate to get away. Maybe, like Odysseus, you will have someone plug your ears so you can continue on to your job, or maybe you'll give in to the cries and stay home to be with your kid. *Either choice is fine*. Do what's right for you and don't feel guilty about whatever you choose.*

*JUST KIDDING, THAT WAS A TRICK, YOU WILL ALWAYS FEEL GUILTY AND UNCERTAIN ABOUT EVERYTHING, SORRY!

60

First Time You Take Care of Your Infant While Sick or Injured

Taking care of a baby while you yourself are sick means doing the work of Marmee from *Little Women* while feeling like Beth.* I woke up one morning feeling like I had both the black plague and dengue fever and possibly also a hangover, the kind where your brain feels like it's sliding back and forth in your skull like a canoe in one of those water-filled novelty pens. I blinked my swollen eyes and pulled the covers over my head, and that's when I heard chirping from the other room.

Oh yes. That baby I had. It wants me.

Surprise! Your baby will not know that you are sick and will not realize that anything is different from any other day. When this happened to me, I summoned every ounce of strength I had to pick up my son and hold him for a few minutes, before allowing him to watch 19 DVDs in a row while I lay in an arm-chair, vomiting.

For those of you who haven't read Little Women, *Marmee (the mother of the March girls) is an insanely strong woman who somehow manages to cook, clean, run a household, do charity work, help with the war effort, and be completely emotionally present while raising four daughters. Beth is the daughter who spends the entire novel in bed, dying.*

TOYS, GAMES, AND OTHER VAGUE ATTEMPTS AT RECREATION

First Time You Realize That Vacationing with a Baby Is Just Taking Care of Her Constant Needs in a Different Place

Have you ever gone on a work trip? Your company flew you to Paris for a convention and you got back and everyone was like, "Oh my gosh, you were in Paris! How was Paris?" and you say, "It was a work trip. I was working the whole time." And some of them accept that, but a few of them will say, "Yes, but you flew all the way to Paris! Did you have a free day? Did you get a chance to do anything besides work?" And you will politely say, "Not really."

Traveling with a baby is like traveling for work. It is great to go places and have adventures and not be afraid of bringing your baby along. But babies, for the most part, need round-the-clock care. When people ask if you enjoyed your vacation, you will not really feel as though you have had one. This is because you haven't. When someone else cares for the baby, it's a vacation. If you care for the baby the whole time, it's a trip.

First Time You Travel Somewhere Without Your Kid and Realize How Amazing It Is

I took a three-week trip to Northern California with a 20-month-old baby and a four-day trip to Los Angeles

without him, and you are going, "I know, I know, I get it, the four-day trip was more relaxing than the three-week trip," and I am shaking my head at you, going, *"The 45-minute subway ride to JFK Airport was more relaxing than the three-week trip."*

First Car Ride Alone with the Baby When He's Screaming His Head Off

Want to get a feel for parenting? Make a recording of a baby hysterically crying* and loop it so it repeats endlessly. Put the recorder in the backseat of your car so you won't be able to reach it while driving and hit play. Now drive somewhere for an hour and a half. When you get out of the car take some sort of psychological test to see whether or not you need to be institutionalized.

If you can't make a recording of a baby hysterically crying, blasting an air horn continually will also work.

First Time Your Baby Accidentally Reprograms the Entertainment System and You Are No Longer Able to Turn on the TV

Children know how to navigate TV remote controls the way people with blindsight are able to navigate long, obstacle-filled hallways. I think the most amazing part about this whole phenomenon is that I am still not sure how to correctly use each of our three complicated remotes, and yet my infant son can somehow switch from A/V input to HDMI 1 while simultaneously taking a dump and eating a Popsicle.

First Birthday or Holiday When Your Child Opens a Bunch of Gifts

Your child is sitting on the floor surrounded by large wrapped boxes, and you and a large group of relatives are standing around her, going, "Open your present, sweetie. Tear open the present! We love you more than anything in the world, and we live in a well-meaning but often consumerist culture! Is anybody filming this? Someone help her with the ribbon!"

Babies do not care about gifts, so do not waste your money. If you absolutely must get gifts for your young baby, below are some inexpensive things that she will absolutely love.

An open box of tissues from which she is allowed to pull out all the tissues one after the other

A roll of toilet paper that she is allowed to completely unspool

Someone's old car keys

Any random picture of a baby

Dryer lint

Those little balls of cat hair and dust that accumulate in the corners of your hallway

The remote to your television or DVD player

Your eyeglasses

Whatever you are holding

66

First Time You Wish People Would Stop Buying Your Baby Gifts

People love buying gifts for babies. Love it. If you are having a baby, people will want to buy you gifts and you will go, "Thanks, gift-buying people! We needed a bunch of stuff for this baby!" much the way Mickey Mouse in *The Sorcerer's Apprentice* goes, "Thanks, magical bucket-carrying broom! I needed this small pool filled up with water!" And you will sit back, so relieved there are people willing to buy things for your child that you will fall asleep with a contented smile, your pointy blue sorcerer's hat tipping forward as your body sinks into your chair. It is only hours later that your eyes will snap open. Wait—is that magical bucket-carrying broom still buying things for your baby? Tell it to stop! *"Stop, broom! That is enough toys! We do not need any more clothes! Stop!"* But the broom will continue to chug along, dropping toys and personalized bean-bag chairs and outfits from the Children's Place, often without a receipt. Eventually you will notice that your once respectable-looking house now looks less like an adult dwelling and more like an exploded Toys "R" Us. You will be touched that you have so many people who love and care about you, and yet you will be unable to thank them, as you will have tragically drowned in a lake of onesies, plush animals, and small trains.

First Time You Realize That Some Expensive Toy You Loved (and Hoped Your Daughter Would Love) Is Ignored Because She Has Fallen in Love with Some $3 Piece of Garbage

Eventually, you (or someone else) will splurge on a very expensive and beautiful item for your child. A bunny hand-sewn by local artisans, perhaps, or an expensive, good-quality teddy bear, or one of those Tree Change Dolls made by that lady in Tasmania who wipes the makeup off Bratz dolls and then repaints them to make them look like ingenue flower children. "What a wonderful thing," you will think. "This toy will become my child's beloved comfort object. She will cherish it!"

No. *You* will cherish it. You will leave it in prominent places, and constantly remind your child it is there. Meanwhile, your child will promptly fall head over heels in love with a synthetic stuffed cat your mother found at a garage sale. Your child will pledge his undying devotion to a plush fox from IKEA. And you will be dismayed that your sweet, innocent child has given her heart to something made of polyester in Cambodia by a child only three years her senior, but that is because you have temporarily forgotten that the most—maybe the only—important thing about a stuffed animal is how much your child loves it. My son has two beautiful, good-quality stuffed

animals, but has given his heart to a particularly absorbent burp cloth. As much as you might want to interfere, let them love what they love. This is probably good advice for when they get older, too.

First Time You Realize You Have Memorized One of His Books

If you are in a conversation with another adult and want to figure out whether he/she has children, casually say the words, "In the great green room there was a . . ." and see if they involuntarily respond, "telephone. And a red balloon. And a picture of . . ." Often they will look startled that they have completed your sentence, unaware that these words are lodged more deeply in their subconscious than most of their childhood memories. I know all of *Goodnight Moon* by heart, despite the fact that after seven years of marriage I still don't know my husband's telephone number.

First Time You Start to Hate One of His Books

I love books more than I have room to explain here, and I was so happy that my child loves having me read to him, because I love reading books to my child.

Except for one particular book that I cannot stand. Ugh, that book. The one I hide under the sofa so he will forget it exists. The one where I regularly skip over pages, hoping he will not notice, in an attempt to make the book shorter. This phenomenon is in no way unique to today's children. When I was a child I regularly requested the 72-page tome *The Cat in the Hat Comes Back,* which, given my mother's response, made me assume the book began with a loud sigh of resignation.

First Game of Peekaboo That Lasts for What Feels Like Forever

Pop quiz! Which of these is the longest?

A The length of time during which a baby will be entertained playing peekaboo

B The song "American Pie"

C All of Peter Jackson's movies played back-to-back

D The Mesozoic Era

(Answer: Dead tie between a and d.)

STOLEN
FROM THE
TRADITIONAL
BABY BOOK

First Smile (That Isn't Gas)

The first few weeks of having a baby are almost completely thankless and feel, frequently, like a relationship where the other person is not pulling his or her weight. The kind where you sit the person down and go, "Look, we've been doing this for two months. I do nothing but tell you how much I adore you. I've given up free time and 'feeling rested' and 'having disposable income,' and all you do is cry hysterically and stare at lamps." And in return your child will slowly fixate on the nearest lightbulb and stare at it for between four and nine minutes.

I was not a huge fan of having a newborn at first because I did not get any of the warm feelings that are supposed to come with it. I felt like the other new mothers had been given golden retriever puppies and I had been handed a miniature version of Tilda Swinton. I would rock my son. Feed him. Change him. Rock him. Desperately try to sleep when he slept. Occasionally cry from feeling overwhelmed. Wonder what other people without newborns were doing. Rock him again. Feed him again. And so on. I loved him, and he was a really good baby, but in general the whole thing felt like when someone recommends a book and goes, *"Oh my god, you have got to read this,"* and you pick it up and get to page 50 or 60 before wondering, "Hey—when does this start to get good?"

For me it got good when he smiled. One day when I was slowly being pulled into an emotional black hole, feeling my *joie de vivre* being absorbed into the emptiness of the cosmos, my child looked up at my face and his mouth turned up at the corners. At first I dismissed it as gas but then it happened again. And again. And lasted for longer. He would look up at my face and he would smile.

I am still not able to fully explain how I felt. It's the sort of feeling that, if possible, should be accompanied by a full orchestra playing music from an inspirational John Williams soundtrack.*

For myself I envisioned the Jurassic Park music from when they first land at the island, but obviously you can pick whatever feels right for you.

First Haircut

Some newborns leave the womb with hair straight from a Whitesnake video, but many children's hair can be *incredibly* slow growing. My own son spent eighteen months sporting an infant version of male-pattern baldness. When a child finally does have enough hair to require a haircut, you can take him to a professional barber (preferably one who has experience with children). Or if you feel like a professional barber is a waste of money, you can do what I did and play a game called Uncertain Mother with Scissors Meets Baby with Rapid, Unpredictable Movements, which is a really fun pastime that (as you can guess) often ends with your child looking as though his hair has been cut by drunk rhesus monkeys.

First Time the Baby Rolls Over

I know this is supposed to be a big one, but how excited can I be over something the dog has been doing effortlessly for years? I'd be way more excited about the "first time baby fetches your slippers" or "first time baby balances a treat on his nose while standing on his hind legs."

First Tooth

Welcome to teething. Teething refers to the several months/ years during which your child's teeth will break through her gums like rows of militant screwdrivers. The downside of teething is that your child will be crying out in pain a lot of the time, and aside from dabbing her gums with a whiskey-soaked washcloth and other strange remedies you hear from people's grandmothers, there's not much you can do about it.* But the upside is that—congratulations—now that your child is teething, you can officially blame *literally every unexplained unhappiness and/or horrible behavior* on her teething. There's a popular theory that Lizzie Borden, Genghis Khan, and Emperor Nero, all of whom are vilified as inhuman monsters, were actually lovely human beings whose molars were just coming in.

If you find that dabbing her gums with a whiskey-soaked washcloth doesn't do anything, I found that dabbing my own gums with a tequila-soaked wash-cloth worked great.

First Time Sitting Up

Your child sitting up will be really, really exciting to *you* because you have been waiting for her to sit up for months and months and (I'm so sorry) not exciting to everyone else. It is similar to telling people what happened in your dreams. You are overwhelmed and ecstatic because you have just come off a wild, magical adventure, and your friend is yawning with half-lidded eyes, going, "That is so fascinating. Tell me more about how you were being chased by the giant penny through a river of melted eyeglasses."

First Laugh

If someone figured out how to take the feeling you get from watching your child laugh and sell that feeling illegally as a street drug, that guy would have a line around the block. Hearing your child laugh is a joyful, ethereal high during which you suddenly can't remember why you were so upset about some pesky forty-five-minute tantrum that happened earlier in the day. Why dwell on the past, right? Children are an amazing, beautiful blessing. You have this nagging memory that possibly you and your partner had a fight about money or that you recently cleaned up a bowel movement more disastrous than the Permian extinction. Did those things really happen? Maybe. It doesn't really matter, does it? I am so overjoyed watching my son laugh that I find myself unable to remember anything that has ever upset me. If my son is laughing and you walk by and casually ask, "Hey, should I have children?" my answer will be an overwhelming, wholehearted *yes*. Yes, you should! Everyone should have children! And it is only later, when the laughter has died down and he is crying because his piece of toast has an eyelash on it that I will be running breathlessly to your door, going, *"WAIT, STOP, I NEED TO REVISE MY ANSWER."*

First Crawl

It can be very exciting when your child is mobile, although not all children will crawl. Many children will scoot themselves with their arms while remaining in a seated position, making them look like small, determined orangutans, and some children will pull themselves along with their upper bodies, dragging their legs behind them like wounded soldiers. Their comfort with mobility progresses *incredibly* quickly as they will start off moving as slowly as my laughable Internet connection and within a week will eclipse the speed of sound.

First Word

You will wait and wait and wait for them to talk, and the longer it takes, the sweeter it will be to hear them say something. You will want so badly for them to speak and suddenly, out of the blue, it will happen and your child will say something. A word. Something incredibly exciting, like "Mama" or "Dada." Your heart will soar! And she will have a second and third word, eventually—things like "cookie" and "bird." It's all moving so fast, isn't it? Those words will lead to phrases such as "The cat is up" and "The dog is outside," which will eventually lead to complex thoughts like "I am sitting in the room" and "I do not want to eat these garbanzo beans," which will then lead to even MORE complex thoughts like "I do not want to eat ANY garbanzo beans, only ice cream," and "Charlotte's mother let her get a tattoo, so how come I can't have a tattoo?" Is everyone's seat belt fastened? You're cresting hills on the roller coaster of development! Her amazingly clear thoughts will segue into dramatic, eye-rolling monologues about how you don't "get it" and you'll never "get it," which will lead to impassioned half-hour tirades about the problem with people in your generation and why she needs to borrow the car. Enjoy your tiny miracle! Welcome to the joy of speaking!

First Step

The journey of a thousand miles begins with a single step. The journey of four city blocks also begins with a single step, but given how many things your child is going to want to stop and look at and touch, the four-block journey will (fun fact) actually take *longer* than the journey of a thousand miles, so good luck making it to her 3:30 pediatrician's appointment.

First Playmate

Your child's first little friend! And by "little friend" I mean "child whose house you will visit to relieve the boredom of being alone with an infant." Often your child will have no more in common with this child than they do with a thermos or a bag of rice. But you will have fun because you will enjoy talking with the other parent (the one who will eventually move away

in milestone 37), and you will say things like "It's so sweet when they play together," which means "It's so sweet when they sit side by side, completely immersed in their own bubbles of thought, occasionally looking up to smile at one another." That is what a young child's "playmate" is. In some ways it's similar to the relationship many adults have with their coworkers.

"IT ALL
GOES BY
SO FAST!"

81

First Time Someone Tells You to "Enjoy It, Because It All Goes by So Fast."

I remember when I had a newborn and people were telling me to "Enjoy this time because it goes by so fast" and I wanted to ask, *"Which part should I enjoy? The exhaustion, the feelings of utter incompetence, or the fact that, thanks to the birth, it will be a minimum of eight months before I can ride a bicycle again? I want to make sure that I am enjoying the right thing."*

As much as you have trouble believing it right now, the time *will* go fast. And as much as other parents have trouble remembering it, the time also goes SO UNBELIEVABLY SLOWLY. *"But how,"* you are asking, *"can time simultaneously move at two different speeds?"* I have no idea! During the one physics class I have taken in my life, I was much more concerned with questions like "When can I get my braces off?" and "If I decorate this denim jacket with puffy paint, will it make me extremely popular?"*

The only thing I can tell you for certain is that even when having a newborn is terrible, people will tell you to "Enjoy it, because it goes by so fast," and each time it happens you have to make the decision whether to say, "You're right, I know it does, I am trying to enjoy every minute," or to start hysterically crying while simultaneously hitting them with a piece of lead pipe.**

*No.
**Still struggling to find some sort of middle ground on this.

82

First Time You Bribe Your Child

Part of the reason children can't hold positions in federal or state governments is because they are extremely susceptible to accepting bribes.

"What's that, Congressman? You don't want to cut taxes or pour more money into the local school systems? *Perhaps this M&M will change your mind?*"

Bribing kids can be a slippery slope. On one hand, I don't want to teach my son that the only reason to pee on the potty is because I'll give him a sticker, but on the other hand, I'd love for him to be potty-trained before his mid-thirties. Whatever you do, proceed with caution.

83

First Time Your Child Says the Word "No"

Like an incredibly predictable Magic 8 Ball, your child is going to learn to say no and is going to say it constantly, regardless of what you are saying. You can say, "Do you want bananas?" and he will say, "No," and you can immediately say, "Do you NOT want bananas?" and he will say, "No" again because he doesn't even care what you asked, he is drunk with the joy of being able to shut you down. This will be the most annoying thing in creation if you are actually trying to accomplish anything, so my best advice is to just continually ask him questions to which the correct answer (or at least the one you are hoping for) is "No."

Here are the ones I use in case you cannot come up with any of your own:

Will Americans ever embrace soccer as passionately as other countries?

Does chewing gum really stay in your stomach for seven years if you swallow it?

Is being hateful or cruel toward people a good way to interact with the world?

Does money solve everything?

Does eating a 13-inch mousse cake in one sitting count as "breaking my diet"?

What about a 24-inch mousse cake?

First Time Your Child Watches Something You Hate on TV

I'm not saying I hate all children's TV shows*—I'm just saying that if there were bull's-eye inserts for my dartboard with the likeness of Calliou or Toodles from *Mickey Mouse Clubhouse*, my hand-eye coordination would rival that of a trained assassin.

I'm not saying it, but I'm clearly hinting at it.

First Time Your Child Refuses to Share

No one wants to have a child who won't share, but I promise you that at some point you will hear crying and find your child clinging to a dollar-store beach ball as if it were a two-million-dollar inheritance. Why? It is hard to understand why children will not share, and also it is not hard. "Let that other boy use your shovel!" I regularly tell my son, while simultaneously letting him know that under no circumstances can he ever touch my laptop. "Give that girl some of your Cheez-Its," I encourage, while eating ice cream behind the shower curtain so he will not see me eating it and want some. You will constantly be teaching your child that it is important to share things, and he will sob and ask why he has to share his toy with that girl, and it is your job to find a child-friendly way of saying, "Because I love you so much and I don't want you to grow up to be a terrible human being whom everyone hates."

First Time Your Child Hits

What is happening? You so clearly remember sitting in a hospital, cradling this tiny, perfect creature with her little seashell ears and her miniscule curled-toe feet and suddenly she's turned into a B-level *Sopranos* character, whaling on some kid at the playground because he's holding the toy stroller she wants. No! This is not how having a kid is supposed to go! She was supposed to grow up to be innocent and kind and warm-hearted toward all living things, like a tiny Fisher-Price Mother Theresa. No, sweetheart, we do not hit!

Don't beat yourself up. Most children hit until someone teaches them not to. The fact that your child hit another kid is less an indication that she's spiraling into a whirlpool of aggression and more an indication that the other kid was holding a really good toy. That's it. I'm sure even a two-year-old Mother Theresa occasionally pushed down another girl when the other girl wasn't letting her read the Bible passages she wanted.*

*Okay, honestly I'm not at all sure of that, but maybe you could set the bar a little lower for your child than Mother-freaking-Theresa.

First Time You Realize He's Fake-Crying to Get His Way

I am amazed when child actors come off as hokey or terrible when most children are SUCH INCREDIBLE ACTORS. If I were a director I'd sit down with the child and go, "Okay, so your motivation for this next scene is that you can see your mother is eating a chocolate croissant and she's not giving you any, so you need to cry realistically enough that she gives in and offers you some. ACTION!" My son turns on the fake tears so regularly I'll occasionally use his "bouts of sadness" to water my plants.

88

First Time You Have a Total Standoff Because He Flatly Refuses to Put on Pants

There is going to be a time when your child will not want to wear pants (or shoes or a jacket) and you will be going, "No, you have to wear pants," and that is when your child will reenact a four-minute Jackie Chan action sequence in which you are the bad guy with the double-breasted suit and the greasy ponytail* and he is the nimble hero, fighting you off using only folding chairs and a stepladder.

"Why is this so terrible?" you will ask, gasping, struggling to hold your child down long enough to get his feet past the waistband. *"Millions of people wear pants every day. YOU NEED TO WEAR PANTS."* You will call in your henchmen, saying something like "Hold him down, boys!" and that is when your child will pull out the moves Neo downloaded to fight agents in *The Matrix*. And if you are waiting for the part of this paragraph in which I explain *why* children do not want to wear pants, you will have better luck waiting for me to explain organic chemistry or the plot of the 2012 movie *Prometheus* or the popularity of jeggings, because I have literally *no idea*.

*Many mornings the greasy ponytail won't even be a stretch for you.

First Time She Refuses to Go in Her Stroller

There are days when it will be so difficult to get your child into her stroller you will wonder if it is in fact a stroller and not the ejection seat from a military aircraft. If given the choice between wedging a screaming child who does not want to be in her stroller back into her stroller or condensing all the matter in the universe into a hot, dense point smaller than a grain of sand, go with the latter because at least it's theoretically possible you will have success.

First Time You Can't Remember Childbirth in Enough Detail That You Consider Having a Second Kid

Oh, good old pregnancy and childbirth. Was it really that terrible? I mean, it hurt, obviously, but it couldn't have hurt that much, right? It definitely didn't feel like you were being hit by a train during a 30-hour ordeal where you briefly wondered if this was what it felt like to die on a Civil War battlefield, and you certainly didn't spend the next two weeks sobbing and wearing mesh underpants lined with a maxi pad the size of a kayak. The entire experience couldn't have been followed by months of sleep deprivation and the loss of all your free time and disposable income. Was all of it really that bad? I mean, there may have been some rough parts, but it couldn't have been *that* bad, right?

STUFF YOU
NEVER SAW
COMING

91

First Time You Realize That 90 Percent of Your Phone Memory Is Photos/Videos of Your Child

My phone is so ridiculously full of photos of the baby that I regularly have to delete photos of the baby so I can make room to take new photos which are also, obviously, of the baby. There are more photos of my son on his first birthday than there are of Abraham Lincoln in his entire existence.

In case you wanted to know exactly how many photos I have taken of my son, out of a random sampling of 300 or so pictures on my phone, here are the only ones that he was *not* in.

Screenshot of inspirational quote I found on Pinterest

Five photos of my husband and me during a three-day trip to Washington D.C.

Random photo of a light fixture some delivery guys broke with the hope that I can use it for insurance purposes

Photo of a pierogi-shaped Christmas ornament I found in an old SkyMall catalog because I wanted to text it to someone

Numerous photos of my dog, but not nearly as many as from before I had my son

Photo of a cookbook page with a recipe for falafel

Photo of my own teeth because I was trying to figure out whether or not I had spinach in them.

First Time You See Another Parent You Previously Would've Judged Harshly and You Just Feel Sorry for Them

"I cannot believe that person isn't capable of controlling their child. Some people just shouldn't be parents."

You've thought that. Almost everyone has thought that, or something similar about some parent they thought was doing a horrific job and, just so you are clear on this, somebody is going to think that about you.

We all parent differently, and it is SO UNBELIEVABLY HARD to be empathetic instead of opinionated, but it is worth doing if it is at all humanly possible. Instead of saying, "Here's someone texting when he should be parenting," or "Here's someone whose two-year-old wouldn't be screaming if she set better boundaries," say, "Here's a guy who's spent all day with his kids and needs to check his e-mail so he feels like a human being again," or "Here's a woman who, if this were a video game, would have only one bar of life left in the upper right-hand corner of her screen." Remember that this is hard for all of us.

First Time You Realize That It Will Be a Long, Long Time Before You Relieve Yourself in Private Again

Using the restroom after having children is as relaxing as urinating in Times Square on Memorial Day weekend. It is loud and uncomfortable and all the while someone with a rudimentary grasp of English is frantically trying to ask you for help with something. Elmo is there and sometimes a naked person wearing a cowboy hat. Do what you need to do, accept that this is your life now, and move on.

First Time You Hand Him Over to Someone You Trust and Take a Relaxing Shower

Having a baby means either only showering when the baby is napping (meaning you get nothing else accomplished), never showering (this is an actual, real option), or bringing the baby into the bathroom with you, which will be almost as relaxing as bringing a stray cat into the shower with you.

The first time my mother came over and said, "Do you want me to watch the baby while you take a shower?" it was like someone had found me wandering for weeks in the desert and offered me a ladle overflowing with potable water. My

mother said, "I've got him. Go shower. Take as long as you need." And if you are lucky enough to have someone say this to you, run to the nearest bathroom, turn on the shower, and stay in there for the next five to seven days.

First Time Your Baby Doesn't Want to be Held by You and Reaches for the Other Parent

Sometimes the baby will favor you and sometimes the baby will favor the other parent, and you will know, rationally, that that is just how things go. But there are times when you'll want to be with your child so badly—just to hold her little fat legs and kiss her adorable cheeks—that the thought of holding her to your chest and having her curl up on you will literally get you through the day. And you'll walk through the door, exhausted but beaming, so excited to spend some bonding time with your baby. Your significant other will try to hand her over to you, and for some reason the baby will scream as though being in your arms is the equivalent of being thrown into a pit of venomous snakes. You'll go, "My baby! I have waited all day to hold you in my arms so that life will feel right again," and for some reason that day your baby will be the bitchy teenager in the middle school cafeteria going, "Ugh, you? I am NOT sitting with YOU." The bonus to this, though it won't feel like it at the time, is that on days when your baby absolutely does not want to be with you, YOU GET

OUT OF WATCHING THE BABY. Do you hear me? You're free! FREE! Read a book! Take a nap! Go binge-watch whatever TV show everyone is talking about. This should totally make you feel better, but most of the time it won't.

96

First Time Doing Something with Your Kid That You Promised Yourself You Would Never Do

Most of us have long lists of things we *swear* we will never do with our children. "When I have a kid I am never going to let him sit in front of an iPad, and I'm never going to raise my voice or lose my temper. I'll never be that parent who just lets him cry, and I'll never be that parent who picks him up the moment he starts crying! I'm definitely not letting him eat junk food, and I'm never going to bribe him to do stuff, and I'll never be looking at my phone when I'm around him because parents who do that are *the worst*."

Quick update on how all that's going. I have raised my voice. I have absolutely been guilty of both letting him cry and occasionally picking him up when I probably should have left him to work through it himself. He happily eats junk food because (spoiler alert) I also eat junk food, and good luck getting your kid to do something you are not willing to do yourself. I am definitely guilty of looking at my phone sometimes, and the only reason we've never put him in front of an iPad is because we do not happen to own one. What you thought you would be like as a parent will inevitably be different from what you will actually be like as a parent in the same way that what you thought you would be like as an adult is different from the adult you have actually become. How many of us followed through on that dream of becoming an adult and immediately eating a full container of frosting?*

Just me?

First Time You Realize the Lengths to Which You Would Go for Your Child

If someone had told you a few years ago that you would stand in a public swimming pool holding someone's vomit in your cupped hands, you might have laughed at them. If *anyone* had told me I would calmly hold the hand of a person who was crapping all over my legs, I would have said no, sorry, you must be thinking of someone else—that is not a thing I would ever, in a million years, do. But you will do things you never could have believed you would do and will give things up you never imagined you could do without.

We are constantly documenting our children's growth with labeled month-by-month photos, but it's not as easy to document our own changes. Not the superficial changes, like the under-eye bags or the increased likelihood of purchasing your entire wardrobe at Marshalls, but the huge changes we never could have predicted. The fact that you will completely restructure your priorities and have to reimagine your sense of self. The fact that your heart will grow exponentially until it is the size of a horrifically overweight cat. The fact that your child will cry and take an enormous dump all over your legs, and your *first thought* will be "He seems so upset. I just really want him to be okay," and it's not until your *second thought* that you'll say, "And maybe I should dry-clean these pants."

First Time You Realize One of Your Parent Friends Has Vastly Different Ideas About Parenting Than You Do

I have a parent friend who has three bumpers, one on top of the other, woven throughout the slats of her daughter's crib. I think she is completely nuts. I also think she is really fun and hilarious, so why dwell on the weird crib thing? She thinks I am nuts because I do not bundle my son up warmly enough when we go out for walks. Another parent friend thinks I am nuts because she thought birth was magical and I thought it was less fun than having teeth pulled. Parents that you really like are going to sometimes have different ideas about parenting. It is always a little weird when you are letting your son eat something off the floor in front of someone you know has a Purell-filled dunk tank installed in his house, but really, in the long run, none of these things is that important.

First Time You Realize That a Specific Version of Your Child Is Gone Forever

Children are a lot like Microsoft Windows in that they are constantly being updated, and usually without your consent. You think of your child as your child, as if they are one static person, but this is not at all what children are like. You will start with this small, indecipherable bag of needs who will coo and stare at ceiling fans and sleep all the time, and that is what you will get used to having, until one day you walk in and that baby will be gone. Just gone. And you will be wondering, "Wait—What's going on. She was right here a minute ago!" But that was a minute ago. Time moves fast. Now there's a new baby that someone left in her place—one who is growing a few teeth or who laughs and eats solid foods. You will cautiously admit that this one is also nice, and you will slowly become attached to this new baby, loving her as much as you loved the old one, only to one day come home to find that this one, too, is gone. And you will want to cry out, "WHO IS DOING THIS—WHO IS WALTZING INTO MY HOUSE AND REPLACING MY BABIES WITH DIFFERENT BABIES? WILL YOU PLEASE STOP??"

But you won't have time to be upset because even though the baby you loved is gone, there is a new baby in its place who needs your care. This one can say a few words—she laughs more often and has a favorite book and a little more hair. And even as you care for her, you know in your heart that in a matter of months, she, too, will be gone. You will let yourself fall in love with her only to have her replaced by an updated model—one who can string together a short sentence or put on shoes without help. And at some point in the future you will look at your child, who at that point will be six or twelve or forty-three years old, and the memories of all the children who came before will come flooding back. Their little teeth. The way their faces looked when they slept and how they collapsed their body into yours when you watched movies together. The way they used to say "skelekin" instead of "skeleton" and "soom" instead of "spoon," and the way their tiny hands would rest on your shoulder while you rocked them. And it's not that you won't appreciate the current model, because obviously you'll love that one, too. It's just that your heart will ache for all the others. You will look longingly at photos of them, remembering how intensely you loved each one and how sad you were when each one disappeared. And you will feel silly sometimes for missing someone who still, technically, exists, while at the same time knowing that no—they don't really exist anymore. Your *child* still exists, but the little girl from the photos is gone.

100

First Time Your Child Says, "I Love You."

If people considering having children wrote out the pros and cons in an organized list format, no one would ever have children. Because there are a billion cons. Children are expensive. They vomit on you. They touch their own poop and then try to put their fingers in your mouth. They restrict your freedom. They strain your relationships. You worry about things you never worried about before, like "Are the schools good in this area?" and "Hey, is she eating broken glass?" They will have tantrums. And will someday be teenagers. If you do your job well, they will eventually leave you.

And the weird thing about the pros is that they are not clear, tangible things like the cons. The pros will be things like "You walk into her room in the morning and she looks up at you and smiles and you are so happy your heart feels like it will explode through your rib cage." Or "He falls asleep on your chest in the rocking chair and the house is totally still and you can feel his tiny heart beating." Logically, it might seem hard to explain how these bizarrely sentimental good things somehow outweigh the never-ending legions of bad ones. But without question, they do.

The first time my son said, "I love you," I was in the middle of changing his diaper. He looked up at me, smiling, and said, "I love you, Mama." And I got teary-eyed and said, "I love you, too, buddy." And even though this is obviously on the pro side of the list, in a strange way I will argue that it is a con as well. Because it can be incredibly painful to love someone this much.

Having a child will be, at times, painful. And frustrating. I regularly feel vulnerable and uncertain of myself—my moods jumping from overjoyed to overwhelmed in a span of time the length of a toothpaste commercial. It is tiring. And scary. And sometimes feels hopeless. *I have no idea what I'm doing.* Would I do it again?

I would.

ACKNOWLEDGMENTS

First off, thank you to Jonathan. You are the best person I have ever met. Thank you for always letting me pull out that weirdly long eyebrow hair you have that's four times longer than any of your other eyebrow hairs.

Thank you to my wonderful editor, Laura Lee Mattingly, who patiently guided me through the editing process with my self-esteem intact and to Elizabeth Yarborough, who first contacted me about the idea of writing this book. Thanks to Allison Weiner and Tonje Vetleseter for their fantastic art direction and to the rest of the team at Chronicle Books: Sara Golski, Tamar Schwartz, Yolanda Cazares, and Stephanie Wong. Thanks to my agent, Erica Rand Silverman, who is fantastic and whose hair always looks amazing.

Thank you to the ridiculously talented Guy Winch, the awesome Brea Tremblay (and everyone in both of her writing groups), the hilarious Jill Twiss, and the incredible Virginia Sole-Smith for your in-depth feedback. An overflowing cargo ship of thanks to Rachael Parenta, Andrea Kagey, Arthur Carlson, and Melissa Friedman for your amazing edits and insights. Tons of appreciation to Katie Compa and Leslie Bornstein, and a thank you the size of North America to the wonderful Sue Funke.

Thank you to Priscilla D'Apice, Rosario D'Apice, and Raquel Maldonado for your constant support, encouragement, and love. Buckets of gratitude to Carole and Richard Friedman for watching your grandson so often, which allowed me to go out and feel like a human being. Thanks to Pam and Karen and to everyone to whom I am related, either by blood or by marriage. I am insanely lucky to be part of two amazing, supportive families. Thank you to all the parents and comedians who support the blog and who allowed me to pick their brains for this book.

To Ben: Watching you grow and learn has been one of the most fascinating things I have ever been privileged to do. I'm not sure I will ever be able to explain to you how much I love you. Thank you.

And thank you again to Jonathan. I know you hate when I pull out that super-long eyebrow hair even though all your other eyebrow hairs are like half an inch long and that one is the size of the St. Louis Gateway Arch. But you still let me do it. You are such a wonderful, talented, inspiring human being and also you are very patient.

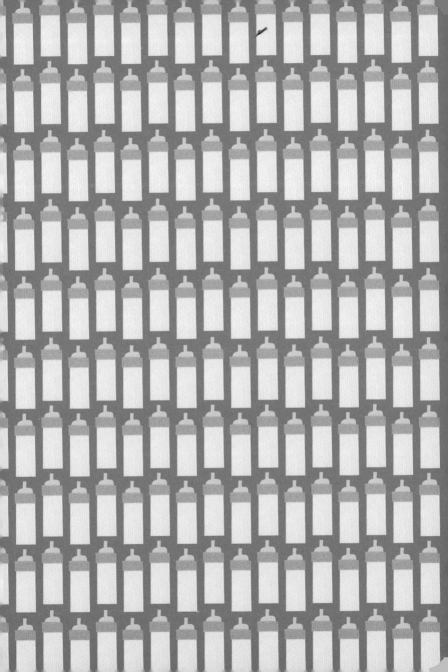

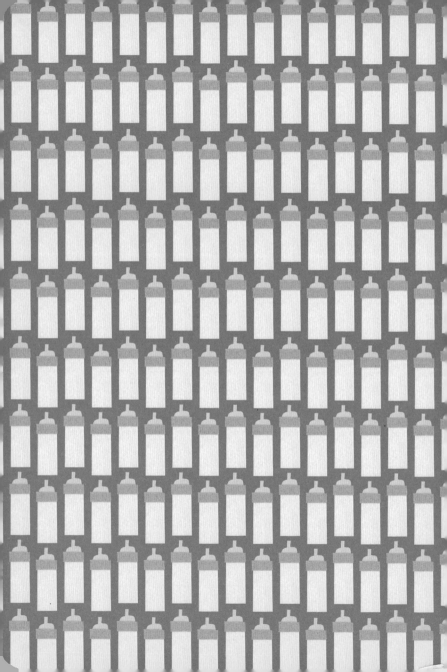